Parallel Peaks:
Business Insights
While Climbing the
World's Highest Mountains

John D. McQuaig, CPA, CMC, CITP

HRD Press, Inc. • **Amherst** • **Massachusetts**

Published by: HRD Press, Inc.
22 Amherst Road
Amherst, Massachusetts 01002
1-800-822-2801 (U.S. and Canada)
1-413-253-3488
1-413-253-3490 (fax)
http://www.hrdpress.com

ISBN: 978-1-59996-070-8

Production services by Anctil Virtual Office
Cover design by Eileen Klockars
Cover Illustration by Sarah Clauser
Editorial services by Andy Dappen, Mary George, and Sally Farnham

Dedication

To Melanie and my kids for enduring and supporting my many passions…

Security is mostly a superstition. It does not exist in Nature, nor do the children of men as a whole experience it. Avoiding danger is no safer in the long run than outright exposure. Life is either a daring adventure, or nothing.

—Helen Keller

Table of Contents

Introduction:
Beginning the Journey

Mountain climbing and running a business: What could those two endeavors possibly have in common? This book will answer that question and, in the process, illustrate there is much about the journey to success that business owners and managers can learn from mountain climbing.

My own experiences have inspired and informed this material. I became an entrepreneur at age 10, mowing lawns for 25 cents an hour. In high school, I had a painting business through which I earned as much money during one week of spring break as most kids earned all summer vacation. I started my CPA firm at age 24. Never content to sit still, I morphed the CPA practice to include a business consulting and coaching practice. I also co-founded North Cascades National Bank. Since the bank's founding 20 years ago, I have served as chairman of the board, enjoying my exposure to many different businesses and industries and watching the bank grow to more than $300 million in assets.

On the mountaineering end, I've pursued climbing for the past 15 years—intermittently scaling mountains throughout the Western United States. I started with Mount Rainier and, in time, managed to climb all the major volcanoes in Washington, as well as two Colorado "fourteeners" (mountains that exceed 14,000 feet in elevation). Overseas, I trekked the heights of Kala Pattar, in Nepal, nicknamed "the top of the world"; its 18,192-foot summit provides a spectacular view of Mount Everest and the 26,000-foot peaks surrounding it. In Africa, I became one of the 20 thousand people who attempt to climb Mount Kilimanjaro each year—and can count myself among the 50 percent whose attempt was successful. In addition, I summitted the third highest peak in North America, Piro de Orizaba, 18,760 feet high, in Mexico.

Interestingly, the success rate for Kilimanjaro parallels that of new businesses. According to the U.S. Census Bureau's Characteristics of Business Owners, two million businesses are started each year in this country, with only half estimated to survive beyond the first five years.

What are the keys to that survival? What prevents the other 50 percent from "reaching the summit"? Are there common principles between running a business and climbing a mountain that illuminate the answers?

One thing I discovered when I started mountaineering is that, similar to business managing, it is a solitary pursuit in many ways. This is certainly true with "trekking"—hiking up a well-marked trail on a smaller mountain—which mainly involves a lot of walking and thinking. However, even technical mountain climbing—a far more dangerous, team-oriented activity—also has solitary dimensions and lends itself well to the comparison with business management.

Technical climbing involves crossing ice fields and glaciers that could include crevasses, or the climber is typically linked to a team of people spread out on a long rope, with no one closer than 60 feet to you. The leader sets the pace and you must keep to it; otherwise, you will tangle your crampons in the rope and damage it. There is a constant, delicate balance between walking on the rope with your crampons and getting pulled up the mountain by your rope mates.

At high altitudes, the team will often climb in darkness, hoping to reach the summit by dawn and get off the mountain before daytime heat widens the crevasses and makes snow bridges more treacherous. Under such conditions, you can rarely even see the person ahead of or behind you. This is a solitary existence. Temperatures can be frigid at the summit, requiring you to bundle up so no skin is exposed—and further isolating you from the world.

Even in daylight, climbing is a solitary endeavor of sorts. There is no one right beside you with whom to exchange looks or carry on conversation. The only connection you have with your teammates is the all-important rope: it is your constant companion, your tether of safety, your lifeline to the world. If you fall into a crevasse or a snow bridge collapses under you, the rope alerts your teammates, who can do a self-arrest to stop your fall and then come to the rescue. Climbing gives you plenty of time to think about the hazards at hand and to brood over the pains and altitude sickness that may be affecting you. It takes tremendous resolve to continue to the summit.

I have found the same to be true in business. Typically, whether you are a CEO, team leader, manager, business owner, or solo practitioner, you have no one with whom to share your frank thoughts about your business or department. You are forced to analyze the situation yourself and constantly reflect on your failures and whatever is standing in the way of the success of your business. This isolation can lead you to abandon the pursuit altogether. On the mountain, it's easy to say, "I'm done," and head down. In business, it's easy to close your doors and give up your dream.

This book is intended to help you hold on to your dream and keep heading upward in your business leadership pursuits. It ties together eight common elements of mountaineering and business management that I have found make a crucial difference between success and failure in either field. The isolation of the business owner or manager sets the stage for some of these components, which together function as "keys to the summit." I am hopeful that the analogies I offer will help you better understand the concepts presented herein and make them easier to put into practice.

Chapter One:
Eight Keys to the Summit

Log: Mount Kilimanjaro, Tanzania, January 31, 2005, 6:50 A.M. (Elevation 18,500 feet, temperature 22 degrees Fahrenheit, windy.)

The occasional crunch of my feet on the loose scree slope is all I hear. Then the inevitable slipping of my foot in the scree. Otherwise, quiet . . . and my thoughts:

> Approaching the "false" summit now. Sun is dawning in the distance . . . eerie red glow flowing over everything. What's that saying . . . "Red sky at morning, sailors take warning"? But we're not sailing, just climbing Africa's highest mountain.

Losing focus. Been climbing this mountain for five days. The last seven hours, the summit push, began just before midnight. No sleep at all last night. Concentrate, focus. People fall and get seriously injured from not paying attention.

Log: Gilman's Point, the False Summit, at 18,651 feet, 7:30 A.M.

At last! When I dreamed of this climb from the comfort of a soft couch, reaching Gilman's Point seemed sufficient. After all, it is on the crater rim, technically Kilimanjaro's summit. Yet I now feel the pull of the "true" summit, the roof of Africa, 700 feet up and a three-hour hike away across the mountain's famous snows. Being the purist I am, how can I possibly stop now?

Still, the utter exhaustion I feel from the steep climb up the last 4,000 vertical feet from Kibo Hut also pulls on me. It's beckoning me down. It makes turning back very attractive. The accumulated stress of the five-day push to reach the false summit wears on me. The elevation wears too: I can only take

*two steps before stopping to catch my breath. I consider all this,
then resolve to take my next two weary steps—they will lead
toward the true summit.*

Log: True Summit Push, 18,850 feet, 9:10 A.M.

*I hike on and notice a climber only a hundred yards ahead of
me. Leaning on his guide for support, he hardly seems to be
moving at all. Finally I notice him stir. His steps advance him
mere inches at a time and require a full-minute pause in
between. To my mind, I'm moving much faster than this fellow,
yet it takes me 45 minutes to close the distance between us.
Humbly I plod by, taking the lead, using my well-rehearsed
pressure-breathing techniques with each step. Several breaths,
one step. Several breaths, one step.*

*Now I am rewarded with a dramatic change of scenery on
the crater edge. The top of Kilimanjaro is laden with massive*

calved-off glaciers, the likes of which I have never seen before. They rise majestically, imposing a surreal scene on me.

Log: True Summit of Kilimanjaro, Roof of Africa, 19,336 feet, 10:45 A.M.

After years of dreaming, seasons of training, months of planning, and five days of climbing, I have reached the top! All of Africa lies at my feet. The feeling is both exhilarating and over-whelming. I share a few high fives with others, snap pictures, eat a snack, and then sit down to rest. Exhausted, my mind wanders. Oddly, what comes to mind is . . . business. It occurs to me that what it took to climb this mountain closely parallels what it takes to run a business.

Since that mountaintop epiphany on Kilimanjaro, I've thought a great deal about the similarities between mountain climbing and business management and what both require for success. Over time, these shared requirements have taken on genuine dimension, developing into eight major components:

1. **Vision:** Establishing and communicating your goal
2. **SWOT analysis:** Examining your situation and its strengths, weaknesses, opportunities, and threats (SWOT)
3. **Planning and preparation:** Thoroughly and diligently readying yourself for the climb
4. **Your own story writing:** Keeping possibilities open and refusing to let naysayers dictate your experience
5. **A supportive team:** Building strength through teamwork
6. **An experienced guide:** Finding at least one Sherpa, literally or figuratively, who knows the territory well
7. **Taking it one step at a time:** Patiently pacing yourself and tracking your progress
8. **Luck:** Realizing that luck is indeed a success factor

This book combines my climbing experiences and those of others with my thoughts about these vital components and their function as keys to success in the business world. The chapters to come focus on the components individually. As a reader, you may choose to explore the topics most relevant to you first or to read the book in order from start to finish. Whatever option you select, be sure to begin with the following overview, which will help you prepare for the greater journey ahead.

The Eight Keys: Overview

1. Vision

In climbing a mountain, your vision is fairly clear. You see yourself standing on the summit. Virtually anything short of that is viewed as a failure. Once you start climbing a mountain, all thoughts and objectives are aimed at reaching the summit.

Most high peaks are shrouded in clouds much of the day, so you can't always see the summit. This was true of Mount Kilimanjaro. Toward the end of the second day of our climb, we saw the mountain for the first time. We had already climbed 7,500 vertical feet, but when the clouds parted, the mountain looked as far away and as high as Mount Rainier looks from Seattle. In short, a long ways away and towering above everything around it! I thought to myself, "I'll never get there!" I had to put these discouraging thoughts out of my mind and remind myself that many other people had done this before me, and that I needed to continue to take it one step at a time.

Vision for a business differs little from the quest for a mountaintop. If your vision for your small business is to grow it to $15 million in sales in three years, the revenue goal obviously represents a summit that you hope to achieve. All the efforts of your stakeholders, including the team, guides, and bankers, must focus on achieving that objective for your company.

The critical element here is to establish your vision and then communicate it clearly to all your team members. One of the advantages of climbing a mountain is that the vision of reaching the summit is obviously clear to all. In business, unless one is intentional about establishing and communicating the vision (your version of the summit), it may not be clear to the company as a whole where you want to go.

2. SWOT Analysis

Once you have your vision established, it's important to do a strengths, weaknesses, opportunities, and threats (SWOT) analysis. This helps you determine what assets are available to achieve your vision, as well as what liabilities may hamper that achievement.

Strengths and weaknesses are typically the *internal* portion of the SWOT analysis. They represent factors you can control. In mountain climbing, these may include your level of cardiovascular fitness, your leg strength, and your general fortitude in the face of adversity. In business, they may be the financial capabilities within the business, marketing, and sales structure, and your personnel.

Since the strengths and weaknesses are internal, you can do something about them. For instance, if you consider your sales force to be a weakness, then you will need to shore it up before you can move toward your revenue goal of $15 million. In addition, you know the bid to reach the summit will require tremendous leg strength and stamina. How does yours rate? Is it a strength or a weakness? What can you do to change it?

A thorough analysis of strengths and weaknesses gets you ready to climb a mountain or run a business. Once you have taken care of those, you must deal with the opportunities and threats, which are *external*.

Opportunities are the positive external factors that could help you. To capitalize on opportunities, you must be aware of them and then jump on them. An example would be a swimming pool contractor who discovers that a 500-lot upscale subdivision is planned in his service area. Once he recognizes the opportunity, he needs to develop a plan to capitalize on it. He may contact the developer and try to work out an exclusive deal for building pools in the subdivision. Maybe contacting the realty agency that has the listing will get him referrals as the lots are sold. He may need to try a number of different strengths to land the work. The fact that he identified the opportunity and recognized its value, however, got him and his team working on a solution to cultivate the business.

Threats must also be considered. They are negative external factors. One common threat in running a business is the rise of new government regulations that may increase your costs dramatically, making your product noncompetitive. In mountain climbing, a storm dumping 20 inches of snow may impede progress or stop you altogether. In both business and mountaineering, you need to position yourself to withstand the threats if they materialize. In short, you need to be prepared by thinking about threats in advance and planning for them.

Conducting an overall strengths, weaknesses, opportunities, and threats analysis is critical to running a business.

3. Planning and Preparation

Both mountaineering and business demand thorough planning. In business, you must think about how to achieve your vision and what stands in your way. The plan needs to shore up your weaknesses, exercise your strengths, capitalize on potential opportunities, and minimize exposure to the threats that could damage the business.

In mountain climbing, you develop a pre-climb preparation plan and then a climb plan. The pre-climb plan includes physical conditioning: you must determine how much aerobic exercise and leg strengthening you need to be ready for the climb. Food and gear selection as well as maps and emergency items should also be considered at this stage.

The climb plan includes how you will proceed once you reach the base of the mountain. It focuses on the route to be followed, how to avoid expected hazards, how to take advantage of possible opportunities, the number of days needed to climb the mountain, and how to get acclimatized to the altitude. The latter is very important because it helps prevent altitude sickness, which is often debilitating and sometimes lethal. When we climbed Mount Kilimanjaro, we stayed an extra night at the 12,500-foot elevation. During the intervening "acclimatization" day, we climbed an additional 2,000 feet and returned to 12,500 feet to sleep. This maximized our acclimatization.

4. Your Own Story Writing

Another shared component of business and mountain climbing is writing your own story. Our guide on Mount Kilimanjaro, Peter Mata, warned us that many people would be telling us their stories of success or failure as we climbed the mountain and they descended. Peter told us to ignore their stories and write our own.

The same is true in business. You'll hear many stories about people whose business ventures failed. Once you are on the road proceeding toward your vision, you are in a position to learn from these stories. But you must remember you're going to write your *own* story regarding your success or failure.

Many successes in business have come from following a path similar to the path that others followed to failure. Ignore the naysayers and write your own story of success if you want to make it in business. If you listen to the naysayers, you may ultimately convince yourself that you cannot succeed.

5. A Supportive Team

The team approach is crucial. In either business or mountaineering, one person can accomplish little alone. In mountain climbing, even successful solo climbers often have a team of people helping them establish the high-elevation camps and supporting them until the day of the summit bid. For the other 99 percent of mountain climbers, a team is the only way they reach the summit.

A team has the shared wisdom to avoid hazards and see opportunities. Together, team members can do the heavy lifting and tedious work. The group effort makes much lighter work for all. A team also provides help in emergencies, such as pulling you out of a crevasse.

In business, teams are also necessary to succeed. Your team may consist of a core of trusted advisors or a league of a thousand employees. In either event, the team propels the business forward. No successful business sustains itself relying on one person alone. Pay close attention to the team's composition and make sure the members are properly trained and work together well to support one another.

An effective business team is generally composed of a diverse group of individuals, each doing their part to move the business forward. The diversity is essential. If you bring together people of varied opinions and talents and engender in them a spirit of cooperation and harmony, the sum of the whole will be far greater than the parts.

6. An Experienced Guide

The next component common to business and climbing is the need for an experienced, well-trained guide or mentor. I have used guides on every major mountain I have climbed. The least experienced of these had climbed the target mountain 110 times and the most experienced had over 600 successful summit bids under his belt. All were invaluable.

Good guides know your location on the mountain at all times, even if the weather deteriorates. They understand the mountain's idiosyncrasies and nuances, including weather, trail, and snow conditions. Competent climbers themselves, they act as independent sources of feedback on how well you are doing, providing perspective on whether you are moving too quickly and risking burn out or moving too slowly to reach the top. They know the medications you may need to take as well as the signs that you are suffering from altitude sickness or other health problems.

With all the variables of illness, fatigue, and weather, well-trained guides recognize when to push and when to back off based on their experience of getting hundreds of clients to the summit. They know countless tricks to help you succeed. For each peak I've summitted, the guide and his team were the principal reason I succeeded.

In business, the need for an experienced guide, consultant, expert, or mentor is just as acute. They can help you see the trail before you, including risks, tax implications, sales issues, industry and economic trends, cash-flow issues, budgeting, and more. You need someone who has seen the ups and downs in business from many perspectives, and who has the experience to help you establish realistic goals and to achieve them. This may be a mentor you have been fortunate enough to meet in your career, a more experienced partner in the business, or a consultant you hire to fulfill this role.

I would never try to climb a major mountain without a guide, and I wouldn't recommend building a business without securing some solid guidance to help you along the way.

7. Taking It One Step at a Time

Without fail, every time I embark on a major climb, I find it daunting simply to approach the mountain. At first sight, such a grand creation seems impossible to climb and surmount. Yet, of course, it can be done—and only be done—by putting one foot in front of the other and taking one step at a time.

On the mountain, it is critical to have a detailed map, a compass, and an altimeter. These tools allow you to chart your progress up the mountain so that you will know how far you have climbed and how far there is left to go.

In business, once you have established your vision or summit, it is important to determine the key performance indicators (KPIs), metrics, or objectives that will designate your progress toward the summit. Together, they become your map and the markings that chart your progress. For instance, if you are trying to achieve $15 million in sales volume in year three, it is important in year one, month six to know where you need to be on sales volume in order to show good advancement toward that goal.

A map, compass, and altimeter will help chart your progress up a mountain. Key performance indicators will track your business progress toward your goals.

8. Luck

Samuel Goldwyn of MGM fame once said, "The harder I work, the luckier I get." In climbing, relentless planning and preparation are the hard work that you hope will produce the results—and get luck on your side. Yet, in the end, you cannot completely exercise control over luck. It has the power to deny you the easiest destination or to grant you the most difficult summit. All the climbing plans in the world cannot keep a freak storm from dropping 18 inches of new snow and making passage to the summit impossible. Luck always plays a role in the success or failure of the endeavor.

Unfortunately, the business world shares this component with mountain climbing and feels the effect of luck every day. For example, business, like mountain climbing, can suffer from bad turns of weather. Think of the ill luck surrounding Hurricane Katrina or the Asian tsunami. Think back through our history to the Great Chicago Fire or the San Francisco Earthquake. Luck can also take a downturn with a suddenly shifting economy, spiking interest rates, or plummeting market demand. Again, preparation can guard against such threats, but in the end, no matter how smart or careful the preparation, luck will have its way. Heightening your level of preparedness in the manner of a mountain-climbing team is usually your best hedge against luck-driven disaster.

Who would have thought my greatest realization at the top of Kilimanjaro would be the eight keys to running a successful business? Not I. But it was, and I would like to share that epiphany in more detail with you, the reader, by focusing on each component in turn in the following chapters. Let's take a look!

The author at 5,895 meters (19,460 feet) elevation—the roof of Africa, the summit of Mount Kilimanjaro

Chapter Two:
The Vision

For something really great to happen, it takes a really great dream!

—Robert Greenleaf

Log: Day three, Kilimanjaro climb, January 29, 2005, 3:20 P.M.

Three days of slogging through the rain forest and through the dry lands surrounding the mountain ... According to the altimeter and occasional signs, we are at the 11,000-foot mark on this 19,400-foot mountain. We've been in Africa for six days and have yet to see the top of the mountain.

Finally, as we come over a rise the clouds lift and the snowcapped summit of Kilimanjaro is in full sight. It's a long, crooked top with snow on the higher end of the crater and no snow at the lower end. It looks 50 miles away and very high and formidable ... It is a glorious sight.

From the moment I first thought about climbing Mount Kilimanjaro, my sight was clearly set on reaching the summit. That was the dream—the vision. Such a clearly defined goal carries a risk because it can blind people to their limitations: it is not uncommon for people to lose their lives trying to reach summits they had no right attempting. Yet that risk is balanced by major advantages, the principal one being that everyone involved in the climb clearly understands the objective: to reach the mountaintop.

Businesses have their own mountaintops. Although you cannot literally stand on those summits, reaching them requires the same clarity of sight as mountain climbing: you must have a vision, one that you can communicate to everyone involved in the endeavor.

Fulfilling this requirement is more difficult in business than in mountain climbing because in a particular business, goals can vary widely. In climbing, you pick a mountain and the goal is simple and direct: you're shooting for the summit—no question about it. Everybody involved, from porters to guides to your family at home, can easily grasp that goal. Reaching the physical top is success; anything less is failure. In business, even the summits themselves must be defined.

Despite this difference, businesspeople can learn a great deal from climbing's inherent clarity of vision and the power that exists in organizing a team around reaching the same goal. Often goals are vaguely shaped in business: the summit is not truly envisioned, or "set." Team members and stakeholders may know they want upward movement, but may be attempting to climb different mountains.

If you don't clearly set your summit, how will you ever know where you're going and whether you're on the right path to success? How will you be able to determine you're making progress? How will you know when you've reached the summit, if you ever do?

In business, we generally refer to the goal, or summit, as the vision for the business. A clearly stated vision answers the question "What are you building?" It places the goal within a time frame: What do you want your business to be in three to five years? It is also succinct enough to be communicated in one statement, commonly known as a vision statement. For example:

> Within the next three years, grow Northwest Electronics into a $15 million revenue company providing wholesale electronic products to retail outlets on the West Coast earning a 10 percent net profit.

This vision statement clearly sets the summit. It tells you where you want to be in terms of gross sales, what types of customers you will be serving in which geographic location, and what your net earnings will be. If you are at $15 million in sales and have achieved these objectives at year two, you will know that you have reached the summit early. On the other hand, if you are at $5 million in sales at year two and have a net loss, you will know how far the summit is.

Although today many companies use vision statements, they do not always ensure that those statements fully and clearly communicate "the summit." It is important to understand what a well-crafted vision statement contains in order to create your own.

Examples of effective, well-constructed vision statements are shown in Figure 1 on the next page.

The Power of a Shared Vision

To understand the power of a shared vision, consider the contrast between two different businesses: Northwest Electronics and Black Jack Enterprises. Northwest Electronics wants a 20 percent growth rate to get to $15 million in sales; it also wants to expand into the

Figure 1.
The Well-Made Vision Statement: Examples

Type of Business	Vision Statement
Social Work	Within three years, grow our chapter of Habitat for Humanity into a sustainable organization building five homes per year for the homeless.
Furniture Manufacturer	In the next three years, grow Hardwoods Furniture into a $50 million revenue, nationally distributed manufacturer providing oak furniture to upscale customers.
Hardware	In the next five years, grow Cornal Hardware into an $8 million retail hardware enterprise serving Southwest Portland from three locations.
Sales Department	Within the next 24 months, build a regional sales department with 24 sales representatives providing coverage in each of our major markets.
Accounting Department	Within 18 months, grow our department to 15 people serving our internal and external customers with state-of-the-art information sources that integrate our financial, operational, customer, and management processes.

Colorado market from its present market in Nevada. The other company, Black Jack Enterprises, has determined they want to grow the company and move forward. Obviously, Black Jack does not have a very clear vision of where they want to go, whereas Northwest Electronics has a tightly defined summit.

What happens with the employees, teams, and other stakeholders in these two companies? Are all the stakeholders aware of what their vision is for the future? The bankers, professional advisors, attorneys, accountants, shareholders, and other major stakeholders should be clearly informed of where the company is headed. Armed with this information, they can help move the company toward the summit.

For example, Northwest Electronics gets a boost when an employee, knowing Northwest is eyeing the Colorado market, spots an article on the rapid growth rate in the Boulder area and shares it with the team. Another employee devises a system that dramatically reduces costs, allowing the company to move closer to their profitability target. Northwest's banker, being fully aware of their planned growth and financing needs, suggests a fixed rate on some level of financing before rates increase so that they can control interest costs. All these contributions are possible because each stakeholder has a clear understanding of where the company is going.

Meanwhile, the other company, Black Jack, not having a clear objective, plunges into the California market without any well-defined strategy for profitability and growth objectives. Their banker—the same as Northwest's—is surprised by the move and put off by the fact that he was not informed of the plan. He schedules a meeting with Black Jack's CEO. The meeting gets testy when the banker asks about this move and the CEO responds: "I thought you knew we wanted to grow. We sensed an opportunity in California and went for it. What's wrong with that?" This spontaneous thinking and lack of planning makes the banker nervous. He worries about what may be next and whether Black Jack is an out-of-control customer—the worst type from a risk standpoint. He also wonders how he, or any other stakeholder, can contribute anything to the company under such conditions.

Black Jack's market plunge soon has the company scrambling for solid ground. The story is different at Northwest Electronics, with whose CEO the banker again meets. He is pleased to see that the company has begun to execute on its plan to move into the Colorado market. The CEO updates him on the progress toward their three-year vision, and he is satisfied that they have experienced only a slight dip in profitability because of the Colorado expansion costs. This had been expected, so it does not come as a surprise. Still, it is good news to hear.

As this example illustrates, it is well worth the time and effort to proceed as Northwest Electronics did and capitalize on the shared vision concept. A shared vision that is clearly defined and articulated is a very powerful tool.

On a personal level, when we have a shared vision of where we are headed, our subconscious starts to work on rooting out information and opportunities that will help us get there. It also works on detecting and dealing with any impediments, actual or possible, between us and our goal.

By way of example, let's say you are considering buying a new car and have finally decided you want a Toyota Camry; however, you can't decide which color to get. As you are driving down the freeway on your daily commute, you suddenly notice many more Camrys than you ever thought existed. You see every possible color combination, too. Are you having a cosmic experience? Not really.

Essentially, you have sensitized your mind, increasing its awareness of Camrys. Thus subconsciously "on alert," you "see" what you have ignored before, producing the data necessary for you to make the color decision.

Now let's consider how this might work for Northwest Electronics. They have 50 employees along with other stakeholders such as bankers, shareholders, suppliers, accountants, and attorneys. If all the stakeholders are clearly aware of the plan to expand to $15 million in sales and move into the Colorado market, their collective subconscious will be on the same "alert," working on the same objective. This magnifies the power of the shared vision. All of these folks will be perceptually sensitive to the needs of Northwest's plans and better conditioned to contribute to its success.

Vision-Setting Methods: Step Method and Summit Planning

Ultimately, visions get translated into sales and profit growth and return on investment, but the numbers come after the vision. In the old-style companies, the numbers are the vision.

—John Naisbitt and Patricia Aburdene, co-authors of *Megatrends*

As we have seen, vision in mountain climbing is not as complex as it is in business, with success more easily defined; thus climbers receive the benefit of a shared vision more naturally as people team up with them to reach the summit. Fortunately, in business there are methods to help you determine your vision. Here we shall look at two in particular: the step method and summit planning.

The Step Method

The step method of determining a business vision is a fairly simple arithmetic equation. What it states is your objective over time. If, for instance, your sales start at $500,000 today and you want to grow them at 10 percent a year, then on a compounded basis, they should be at roughly $732,050 in five years. The final point is really an algorithm, not a vision. It is simply increasing your sales at an inflationary rate plus some historic growth rate.

Businesses often rely on the step method, and as a practicing accountant, I contribute in part to that reliance. Accountants tend to look at things on a numerically conservative basis; thus if we can go back and show that a company has grown at 10 percent annually for the past five years, we wonder why it shouldn't continue growing at 10 percent annually in the future. We can then set a reliable "vision" for the gross revenue five years from now.

The tidiness of that vision is convenient but points to the problem with the step method: the method ignores how your company may actually grow and what new or presently unexplored opportunities will come into play in the future. Moreover, most companies do not grow in truly consistent steps. For a more accurate picture of such growth, we must turn to summit planning.

Summit Planning

To reach the summit of a mountain, the initial objective is clear and unambiguous: it's either the 14,410 foot summit of Mount Rainier or the 29,035 foot summit of Mount Everest. The mountain is the mountain. The summit is the summit. And only in very rare instances like a volcanic eruption does the height of the summit change. As a result, the vision is clearly established by the summit. The unambiguous summit is a huge advantage in mountain climbing.

Summit planning involves three main steps: the first is defining where you are today, the second is defining where you want to be, and the third is determining the bite-sized steps needed to get you there. The result in step two is your vision—the summit. The result in step three is your strategy for success; it provides you with a set of milestones or metrics for tracking your progress toward the goal.

With the summit clearly established for mountain climbers, the issue becomes strategy on how you reach that summit. Mount Everest has several famous approaches to it, and for any expedition that hopes to reach the top, the strategy and plan will vary. As a climber, you may decide to take the more difficult northeast ridge to reach the summit. As a less-experienced climber, you may want to take the well-traveled "Hillary Step Route" that results in a slightly higher level of success. In either event, your paths and elevations will vary at any point in time, but both strategies may result with you at the summit.

In either business or climbing, you must be thorough as you work on step three—your strategy for success. There are typically a number of different paths or strategies to get you to your vision, and not all of them are necessarily equal. For instance, let us return to Northwest Electronics and its goal of reaching $15 million in sales. The company's strategic options for success might include:

- Expanding into the California market
- Buying out a competitor
- Raising additional capital to start new operations in other markets

Northwest will need to decide which option is best for it at present.

Northwest Electronics Summit
$15 Million in Sales

Whatever steps you choose to reach your summit, it is unlikely that progress will occur in a straight line or at a strictly even pace. Your path may lead straightaway to the summit. In actuality, "straight" is a relative concept, with one strategy promising a more direct path than the others. Also, the pace of progress toward the summit can be greatly boosted by new opportunities. For instance, suppose Northwest sees an acquisition opportunity, takes it, and consequently experiences a big jump in sales. It has also "jumped" closer to its goal. In such cases, growth is likely to become more consistent in the aftermath, based on the new, higher plateau the company has reached.

Deciding Which Visioning Method to Choose

Your choice of method will depend on many factors, but essentially, you need to ask yourself, "Do I want to stay in line with the existing market for my business, or do I want to go beyond that?" Most likely, the step method will not help you leapfrog your way into a higher market share or gain greater scale and presence. In fact, it probably will not get you any additional market share at all.

If, for whatever reason, you desire to grow to a certain size, you will do best to consider the truly visionary summit planning approach. For example, let's say that you have 20 percent of your market and know that having 35 percent in three years would give you better market access and control, better relationships with your suppliers, and more strength as a marketing force in the marketplace. In such a case, you do not want to employ the step method, which cannot support this type of extraordinary growth or help you strategize the way to the summit.

Summit planning is readymade for your purpose. It will help you justify your purpose and clarify your strategies, such as the need to roll up or purchase a few smaller operators in your market. This clarity of vision will be indispensable when it comes to negotiating with potential purchase targets. You will be able to share with them your vision for growth and why it is necessary, thus increasing their motivation to sell to you. They will better understand the reality of the marketplace and the need to grow in order to prosper.

That said, the step method does have a place in vision setting as a good way to test the vision you have established. For instance, if Northwest Electronics wanted to grow its sales to $15 million from a current level of $1.5 million, they would need a huge infusion of capital and have to take a number of major steps toward increasing revenues. Incrementally, meeting the goal would require a growth rate approaching 60 percent per year. Using the step approach, the company could go back and test the vision to see whether this is possible.

In short, the step method is a pathkeeper. It can give you a fairly safe path toward your vision or send you back to redefining that vision and, ultimately, your strategy for how you get to it. Don't let yourself get lulled into using this method alone. Also, don't forget that it can be an effective tool when combined with summit planning.

Chapter Three:
Working Up a SWOT

"To give style" to one's character—a great and rare art! He exercises it who surveys all that his nature presents in strength and weakness and then moulds it to an artistic plan until everything appears as art and reason, and even the weaknesses delight the eye.

—Friedrich Nietzsche

Although men are accused of not knowing their own weakness, yet perhaps few know their own strength. It is in men as in soils, where sometimes there is a vein of gold which the owner knows not of.

—Jonathan Swift

Whenever I decide to climb a major mountain, I always conduct a SWOT analysis anywhere from three months to a year before the climb. This analysis of strengths, weaknesses, opportunities, and threats is more like a snapshot in time, but if it's detailed and comprehensive, it gives me a good idea of what I need to do from a strategic standpoint to prepare myself for the climb ahead.

The same concept applies to business. Doing a SWOT analysis gives you a good idea of where your company stands today and what changes must be made to reach your "summit." You can use this strategic planning tool with virtually any kind of business or company department, and should consider it an essential part of your "climbing equipment."

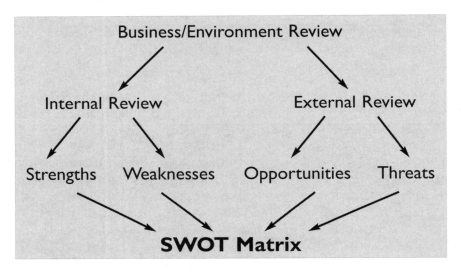

The analysis itself consists of a scan of your company's internal and external environments. Internal elements are examined and then classified as either strengths or weaknesses:

- **Strengths (S)** are the areas of high performance. You identify what you're doing well and how you can further strengthen these areas.

- **Weaknesses (W)** are the areas of low performance. Once you identify these areas, such as too much wastage and lost production time, you can develop strategic measures for improvement.

External elements are also examined and classified as either opportunities or threats:

- **Opportunities (O)** are circumstances or situations advantageous for your business to pursue or factor into planning. For example, analysis may show that you have a chance to improve your market share in a growing market.

- **Threats (T)** are signs of possible or impending danger to the business. Examples of threats include a new product that could directly compete with yours and new legislation that will adversely affect your industry.

When these elements and their examinations are combined, the result is your SWOT analysis.

Strengths and Weaknesses: Looking Within

Because the strength and weaknesses portion of the SWOT involves looking within the business, you are on familiar ground. These are the variables you can *directly control.*

Strengths

A company's strengths are its assets and resources that it can build upon to strengthen its competitive advantage.

Strengths may include the following:

- Patents
- Entrepreneurial culture
- Well-established teams
- Well-documented systems and processes
- Excellent reputation among customers
- High profit margins
- Well-diversified product mix

Weaknesses

Weaknesses for a company may be the absence of a strength or a documented internal problem.

Examples include the following:

- Negative profit margin or losses
- Hierarchical, stodgy culture that reacts slowly to change
- Manager/Owners in poor health with no succession plan in place
- Lack of a cohesive marketing strategy
- No clear vision

Generally a weakness is the converse of a strength. A strong marketing plan is a strength while lack of a clear marketing strategy and plan is a weakness.

The internal components of a company can be broken down into several specifics:

- Vision
- Strategy
- Structure
- Culture
- Products and services
- Marketing and sales
- People
- Systems and processes
- Finance

Vision

Chapter 2 addressed the vision in detail. The importance of the vision cannot be overemphasized. To clearly identify what steps you need to take to be able to reach your summit, you have to define your summit. For your business, that may be reaching a

sales level of $15 million in three years with a net margin of
20 percent. This clearly defined vision allows you to see where
your business is headed.

Strategy

Strategy helps you take aim toward your vision. For instance, if
you are aiming for a 20 percent net profit margin, you may need
to strategically target companies exceeding $5 million in revenue
in your sales and marketing. This "strategy" will ensure that the
customers you solicit and ultimately land are capable of paying
for your services.

Structure

Structure represents the departments and personnel that need
to exist within the organization to support the strategy and vision.
Let's say, for example, that your strategy calls for excellent customer
service through proactive customer contact and immediate response.
For this to happen, you would need a well-designed customer service
department staffed with adequately trained individuals who understand your products and the needs of the customers. They will also
need to have the time to support the strategy and ultimately the
vision of the organization.

In summary, the structure is the sum total of the organization
chart—the people and processes necessary to execute the strategy
and deliver the vision.

Culture

The culture of a business can be defined as the sum total of the
beliefs, values, and behavior that characterize the business. A
business or department typically has a collective culture that
overrides everything that it does.

For example, a particular business may have a culture that allows it to react quickly to changing circumstances. Such a culture can be a strength in that the company is light on its feet and able to change quickly as circumstances change. Its people do not get stuck in an endless analysis of information, but rather react and make decisions and changes as a result.

By the same token, a culture like this can be a weakness if the company reacts too quickly to changing circumstances. The lack of analysis and the force of overreaction can lead to consequences that are worse than if the company hadn't reacted at all.

Products and Services

Your products and services component is the collective of the individual products and services that your company offers. In the automobile industry, your products would be all the various automobiles, trucks, and sport utility vehicles that your company has available. If you are in the service industry, it would be the individual services that you offer.

As you analyze your products and services, you need to look at the strengths and weaknesses of each. You also need to consider the product life cycle of each. In addition, it is worthwhile to consider what product extension you may be able to bring to your existing customers.

For instance, General Motors identified a need for people to get help when stranded on the highway. To respond to that need, the company developed OnStar as a service it could sell to buyers of GM products. OnStar service provides these customers with a built-in communication system in their vehicles. Should an emergency arise, they can simply push a button to connect with an operator who can coordinate emergency services. OnStar not only provides an additional revenue source for GM, but also helps generate additional vehicle sales because of its exclusive availability to GM products. That is a great example of product extension to existing customers.

Marketing and Sales

To get a good idea of where you stand in the marketing and sales area, you will actually need to conduct a series of evaluations. At a minimum, this should include evaluating the following:

- Your marketing plan
- The quality of your existing sales channels
- The quality of your salespeople
- The quality of your results
- The regularity with which you track key performance indicators on sales

By organizing your analysis in this fashion, you are in a better position to spot weaknesses. For instance, if you find that you have a reasonable marketing plan but a failure in one of your sales channels, you can make changes in that sales channel and get things back on track.

For a more concrete example, let us say you own a small regional winery. With the proliferation of new wineries in the country, you find it's difficult to get your label recognized and marketed within the retail channel, and sometimes even more difficult within the wholesale channel. You thus need to carve out a niche for yourself. You conduct an evaluation series and realize that on the retail side your wholesale distributor is not producing much traffic and that you don't have a winery location for consumers to visit. You see that you must look into other marketing channels, such as a wine club, newsletter, and catalog distribution. The possibility of creating a destination that people would want to visit to purchase your wine also does not escape you. Because of your series of evaluations, you now have ways to improve your marketing and sales.

People

Do you have adequate people resources to move you toward your vision? Consider your organization chart and what gaps may exist in it. For instance, if you are in an information-based business but don't have adequate information-technology people, at some point you will hit the wall and not be able to progress further without enhancing that component.

It is thus essential to take a proactive look at your people resources and determine whether they are adequate to move you toward the goal. If they are not, you must fill in the gaps.

Systems and Processes

In my work with small businesses over the past 30 years, I have seen the lack of systems and processes as one of the biggest detriments to consistent performance and success.

A system or process is the documenting and defining of the actual processes that take place in your business. These may include the operational processes of how you inject the mold to build a plastic part for a product or how you document conversations with clients. It could also cover administrative processes like collection of accounts receivable.

When Ray Kroc developed and franchised the McDonald's restaurants, he recognized the importance of systems and processes. McDonald's now has highly systematized methods, which means it can hire significantly fewer experienced people and still get consistent results in the end. Because Kroc had a vision of thousands of restaurants putting out a consistent product, it was important that systems and processes be clearly in place, that employees be given training, and that product consistency be tested.

It could be argued that the true value of McDonald's franchises is the systems and processes that come with them, not necessarily the marketing trappings or name recognition. Most people who are buying a franchise are buying the systems and manuals that accompany it.

Because consistent performance is so critical to success, it's vital that small businesses document the systems and processes they use. Keep this in mind as you analyze your SWOT, and be sure to consider the existence and documentation of all systems and processes within your business.

Finance

Finance in particular is one part of your internal engine that must be clearly evaluated. Many a business with strengths in the other internal areas—products and services, marketing and sales, people, and systems—has fallen from grace and into bankruptcy from the lack of adequate financing. In short, without the financial capital to deliver on your vision, you will go nowhere.

Many entrepreneurs assume that because their business is currently growing and increasing in sales and profits, they can rest assured the business will be successful in the future. But generally, a growing business sucks up a lot of working capital for necessities such as accounts receivable, inventory, and equipment purchases. The end result is that many growing "successful businesses" actually fail because they don't have the appropriate finances in place to support their vision in the long term. It becomes impossible for them to grow and capitalize on their initial success.

Often, by the time you realize that your capital is insufficient, it's too late to access the finances needed to keep your business going. This "cylinder" is thus vital to analyze and deserves your utmost attention in terms of maintenance.

Be Prepared—and Realistic

A strengths and weaknesses analysis will be worthless to you if, at the start, you believe there cannot possibly be anything wrong with your business. You must be realistic. Don't kid yourself about any weaknesses revealed by the analysis: you're not going to improve those weaknesses if you don't acknowledge them. You may want to include your employees or other stakeholders in the feedback loop for the SWOT input.

Also, don't be surprised if your list of weaknesses is much longer than your list of strengths. It's not unusual. In my experience, when we take an exhaustive look at the workings of most small businesses, we see a lot of weaknesses. Be prepared to recognize the problems that you find and to work toward improvement.

Opportunities and Threats: Looking Outward

In conducting an opportunities and threats analysis, you must consider the wider business environment around you. In this context, it's useful to think of a business as a cork on the ocean. When the tide goes up, the business goes up; when the tide goes down, the business goes down. When a storm strikes, the business gets swept in whatever direction the winds take it. Essentially, it gets buffeted by the various external changes occurring around it.

The external business environment falls into several categories:

1. Industry conditions
2. Competition
3. Technology
4. Customers
5. Shareholder circumstances
6. Economic environment
7. Suppliers
8. Social changes
9. Political and regulatory environment

In the balance of this chapter, we will look at each of these categories and the related questions they prompt us to answer.

1. Industry Conditions

The questions:

- *What's happening in the industry you are a part of?*
- *What kinds of changes are occurring?*
- *Is the industry growing or contracting?*

These days, changes in most industries are happening at an accelerated pace. For instance, think of cyclical industries like residential construction. The industry cycles up and down based on such factors as interest rates and local or regional economic environments. The end result? Conditions within the industry have a significant impact on individual homebuilders and how well they fare.

The critical element is positioning your business—considering industry conditions—for the changes that will inevitably occur. Cyclical changes in most industries are guaranteed, and you need to prepare for them.

2. Competition

The questions:

- *Who is your competition now?*
- *Who might become your competition?*
- *How can you get "under the radar screen" to detect who is rising as a competitive force?*

Many businesses are not aware of who their competitors are or could be. They may watch the obvious competitors, but neglect to think about the ones under the radar screen or the up-and-comers. It's a dangerous way to run a business.

Take Motorola in the early 1990s. They owned the cellular phone business in the United States and were entirely committed to the analog cellular phone. Nokia, a Finnish company that made rubber boots and snow tires, saw an opportunity in the digital cellular phone revolution and swiped the lead in market share from Motorola. Originally, they had no position at all in the cellular phone business; today they're the worldwide leader. Motorola did not properly assess where their competition *might* be coming from and therefore lost their market-leader position.

When you analyze your competition, think about the obvious competitors and then brainstorm who potential new competitors might be. The best sources of information on competitors might be industry trade groups or your own customers.

3. Technology

The questions:

- *What technological changes now occurring could make an impact on your business?*
- *Is technology your enemy or your friend?*

I had a client who owned a travel agency in the early 1990s. The agency had a large base of customers, corporate and individual, who relied on its services for their travel-planning needs, including airline reservations. All was well until customers began buying home computers—and discovered the Internet. They realized they could make their plane reservations themselves at the big airline sites. This was more convenient than using a travel agent and gave them a feeling of conquest when they nabbed a good deal. Soon Expedia.com and Priceline.com offered them a chance to bid on airline tickets and hotel reservations and get even better deals to brag to their friends about. The digital revolution had arrived, and my travel-agency client was entirely unprepared for it.

In a relatively short period of time, my client's customers had an entirely different distribution channel available to them—the Internet—and they were choosing to use that instead of her agency. In this situation, survival demanded change. Some agencies were able to meet this demand by switching to an effective Internet distribution model. Many others that carried on with business as usual died as demand for their services dried up.

What is the message behind this example? You must keep abreast of technology and be on alert for any changes or innovations that could affect your business, whether directly or indirectly. Remember: the Internet began as an information tool accessible to a few, but with further innovations swiftly became a revolutionizing business tool accessible to all.

To make sure you don't get left behind in technology's dust, answer the following questions now and return to them regularly in the future:

- What impact does technology have on your business, and how will it affect your future?
- Are there opportunities for you to lower cost and get closer to your customer through technology, or is it really not applicable to your business at present?
- If technology isn't applicable to you now, are there any ways it could become applicable?

Keep in mind that tech-related business innovations that seem threatening can actually afford you promising opportunities if you're on the alert. Here are two examples:

- Local independent bookstores were hit hard when Amazon.com started distributing books over the Internet; however, used bookstores in the know made gains because they were able to post their inventories on Amazon's website. Today when you search for a book at Amazon.com, you are given both new and used book options throughout the country.
- Web linking and marketplacing have allowed competing businesses to work out mutually beneficial alliances. For

example, a recent book search of mine at Amazon.com revealed not only Amazon's price and book edition, but 132 sources for the book at various prices and editions. One of the sources was Powell's Books of Portland, Oregon. Although Powell's has its own website, it has done what it takes to get its inventory of thousands of new and used books available through Amazon's marketplace. It thus gains an alternative, popular channel for reaching customers through a competitor who itself gains financially from marketplace fees and commissions.

4. Customers

The questions:

- *Who are your customers?*
- *Are they able to purchase your products without financial strain?*
- *Are your products discretionary or primary purchases for them?*
- *What is happening to your customers economically today?*
- *What might happen to them?*
- *How well do you connect with them and their wants and needs?*
- *Are there any new trends that might influence their buying choices?*
- *Are there any new or potential necessities that might influence their buying?*
- *Are there any demographic changes on the horizon that might have an impact on your customer base?*

Customers and their cash flow are the lifeblood of any business enterprise. In today's fast-paced and changing environment, it's critical that a business be acutely aware of what its customers are thinking. What's happening to those customers? Are their economic prospects increasing or declining? How well do you connect with your customers?

To be successful, you must create a customer-focused organization. Focusing on customers and their wants and needs is what can give your company a true competitive advantage. The more customer information you have, the easier it is to integrate their needs into your products or services. And don't forget the information you must provide to customers: from their perspective, customers should know from your mission statement precisely why you exist.

As you look at customers, carefully consider *why* they need your products or services. When Henry Ford first developed the Model A, there was one Ford model available in one color (black), with one engine and virtually no options. Over time, the automobile industry has realized that cars are not only about transportation; they are also—if not more so—about extending our personalities and egos to the cars. As a result, we now have a plethora of options available for cars, and most vehicle marketing is aimed at satisfying some "need" other than transportation.

The next time you see a car commercial on TV, pay close attention to what you're being told about the vehicle; that will probably be very little. Most of the sales pitch today focuses on how the car will make you feel—how free you will feel, how strong you will feel, how important you will feel. The marketers have definitely figured out that cars are not just about transportation. They fulfill many other "needs" of their owners.

You should also consider any demographic changes that may affect your customer base. Is that base growing or shrinking? Keep in mind that not all demographic changes will have an effect. For example, I've been involved with the building committee for our local school district. Our "customers" are the elementary students. Although our community has grown in population, the number of those customers has not grown. Why? Because along with the population growth, part of the community shifted from an agricultural area to an upscale suburban environment; it turned out that the agricultur-ally based portion of the community had far more elementary-aged children per capita than did the suburban portion.

5. Shareholder Circumstances

The questions:

- *What is the current status of your shareholders?*
- *Are they financially strong?*
- *Do they have a continuing interest in supporting the business?*
- *Do they have additional funds available for company financing needs that might develop?*
- *Are they relatively young, healthy, and able to continue to work and support the business in the future? Or conversely, are they ready to retire and get out of the business?*
- *Do they have competing demands for their capital, making it difficult for them to support the business?*

The shareholders are external to the business, and you need to separately evaluate what kind of support they bring to the endeavor. Consider their circumstances carefully. I have dealt with all types of shareholder circumstances over the years and can assure you that they are important.

Small public companies, to the extent they can be aware of these circumstances, need to understand them and plan accordingly. Such a company may have someone accumulating its stock with the intention of forcing a sale of assets or gaining a board seat. Family or closely held companies are often significantly affected by shareholder needs and circumstances. For example, a major shareholder may suddenly die, forcing a sale of the business. In any business, it is possible a minor shareholder will get fed up with his or her lack of control and persuade other shareholders to help take over the board.

What is the attitude and circumstances of your shareholder group? Are they in for the long run with adequate capital to invest, or are they ready to sell and move on?

6. Economic Environment

The questions:

- *What's occurring within the economy and business environment you serve?*
- *Are business incomes growing or declining?*
- *Are the incomes of the population growing or declining?*

Another element of the external framework is the business environment, which can have an enormous impact on your success. For example, in the early 1970s, Boeing cut its Supersonic transport (SST) program and, with a shrinking demand for workers, also cut more than half of its work force in a year's time. This meant the loss of over 40 thousand jobs and sent Seattle's business environment into rapid decline. With people caught in an economic slump and unable to spend money, there was little that businesses could do other than focus on other geographic markets. A city billboard summed up the dire situation: "Would the last person who leaves Seattle please turn out the lights?" Once it gets to this point, it may be too late to save your Seattle-based business.

Is your company at risk because of its geographic concentration? Can you diversify it before a calamity like this hits?

7. Suppliers

The questions:

- *Do you have significant suppliers that provide a majority of your goods or services?*
- *Are your suppliers strong or weak?*
- *Are your suppliers leading the industry or lagging behind?*

The condition and attitudes of your suppliers can have a huge impact on the success of your business.

The extreme case has a business wrapping its entire existence around a single supplier. Consider a Ford car and truck dealer. The results of the dealer are heavily impacted by the success, or lack there of, of Ford Motor Company.

If Ford's products are well positioned in the marketplace and lead the industry, then the dealership has a chance to be successful. If not, even a dealership with a lot of internal strengths will have a hard time being successful.

Many dealerships that identified this type of threat compensated by purchasing or opening dealerships of other brands. Most automobile dealership businesses now own franchises for several brands to diversify their product mix and supplier mix.

Consider how tied your business is to a single supplier. Are there ways to diversify your product and supplier mix?

8. Social Changes

The questions:

- *Are changes in social norms bringing customers to you or driving them away?*
- *Are social considerations affecting the public perception of your business?*
- *Are health concerns causing customers to reconsider your products?*

The social environment has a huge potential to affect the outcome of business operations. The effect can be positive or negative.

I have owned Ribbon Cliff Orchards, LLC, since 1985. The orchard produces apples, cherries, and nectarines. Over the past 20 years, the social attitude toward food consumption has changed dramatically.

Most recently, more people have decided to limit the amount of unnatural chemicals they consume. As a result, the market for organic produce has grown exponentially in the United States.

In 1995, as owner of the orchard, I considered these social trends along with other facts:

1. The Department of Agriculture requires a three-year transition period for an orchard to move to organic production.
2. Production costs of organic orchards are one and a half times as high.
3. Organic fruit at that time sold for a 30 percent premium.
4. The supply and demand situation for organic produce was tenuous.

Considering these and other factors, I decided to switch 80 percent of my production to organic. The transition period was tough. I had all the additional costs without the additional revenue.

Ultimately, the social drive for organic produce continued to increase. This drove demand higher.

Today organic varietal apples sell for a 50 to 70 percent premium and my decision to switch to organic looks like a winner.

From my own personal social perspective, it feels good to be finding more carbon-based natural methods of farming.

9. Political and Regulatory Environment

The questions:

- *Is Congress or your state legislature considering legislative changes that would impact your business?*
- *Are regulatory changes in the hopper that could affect your business?*
- *Is the Securities and Exchange Commission considering changes to reporting requirements for your business?*

I have many clients who complain that regulatory and legislative changes are their biggest threats. Collectively, they are uncontrollable and can inflict damage from minimal to catastrophic. By the same token, these changes can also drive positive results in a business.

The well-publicized Sarbanes-Oxley (SOX) Act that greatly increased reporting requirements for publicly traded companies drove double-digit growth for large accounting and audit firms.

SOX has also caused many smaller publicly traded companies to reconsider that status. With the additional costs of SOX compliance running in the low six figures at a minimum, some small publicly traded companies have elected to buy back stock and go private to save the costs.

Legislative and regulatory changes can have a huge impact. Carefully consider this area.

Developing a Strategic Plan

Once you've completed your SWOT analysis for the business, what do you do with the information? You develop a strategic plan to build on your strengths, compensate or improve your weaknesses, capitalize on the opportunities available, and protect yourself from threats.

You can build on your strengths by matching them to opportunities in the marketplace. For instance, a company with a very strong product that has good market share in the Northwest region might decide to develop distribution channels into the Southwest region, which is a rapidly growing part of the country. The company could thus capitalize on that strength by realizing the economic opportunity that exists in the new region and move forward.

If your analysis shows that you have looming cash flow problems, you might decide the answer is to pursue marketing opportunities and maximize sales in the short term by discounting. This, of course, means that you're going to reduce your profitability on each sale, but try to increase your gross sales. A short-term strategic decision like this may be helpful—or disastrous. It can cause your receivables to balloon and, ultimately, not provide the profitability that's going to return the cash to the business. You need to carefully analyze strategies like this from all angles.

The value of your SWOT analysis and what you have uncovered about your business can be immense; but without an effective strategy for addressing the weaknesses and threats it reveals, you will undermine that value. You must select your plan carefully, identifying the best strategy for your needs, and then develop the plan judiciously. Strategy identification can be difficult. However, if you ensure that you understand the SWOT results for your entire business, you will be in a better position to judge what is necessary to move your business closer toward the "summit."

Chapter Four:
You Can't Prepare Too Much

A goal without a plan is just a wish.

—Antoine de Saint-Exupéry

The reason most people never reach their goals is that they don't define
them, or ever seriously consider them as believable or achievable.
Winners can tell you where they are going, what they plan to do along
the way, and who will be sharing the adventure with them.

—Denis Watley

In 1963, Sir Edmund Hillary was the first person to reach the summit of Mount Everest. He had a carefully crafted plan in place to achieve that goal. It consisted of five parts:

1. **The vision for the plan.** That vision would be to reach mountain's summit. Pretty simple!

2. **The mission.** This would be his purpose and reason for the endeavor. Considering that no one had yet conquered Everest's summit, the earth's highest point, it's likely there was much more to Hillary's motivation than the mountain simply "being there."

3. **The objectives.** These would be his measurements, in place. The measurements would tell him how he was doing and allow him to track his progress as he worked toward his vision.

4. **Strategies.** What would he need to reach the top of the world? He would need Sherpas and the local labor force to ferry his gear to the base camp and the various high camps above that. He would also need Sherpas and others with local climbing experience as guides. To deal with the political challenge of securing permits, he would have to get his embassy involved.

5. **An action plan.** Precisely what steps were required to reach his vision? Those steps would run the gamut from getting into appropriate physical shape to building a first-class climbing team.

Hillary's success at his endeavor—a feat that, at the time, seemed impossible to pull off—is a testament to the power of such planning, and offers a major lesson to business owners and managers: in business, just as in climbing, there is no more important key to success than having a well-documented and well-executed plan.

Fortunately, businesses have available to them a useful planning tool that incorporates all the elements that Sir Edmund Hillary needed for success. That tool is The One Page Business Plan®, for which I am a certified consultant. It was developed by Jim Horan, who presents the tool in his acclaimed book *The One Page Business Plan: Start with a Vision, Build a Company!* (2004). Horan's work has made many other planning strategies obsolete, and will guide this chapter's consideration of the all-important business component of planning.

Why One Page Can Get You to the Summit

The classical business plan is an involved, in-depth treatise that is "published" and then put on a shelf to yellow and gather dust. In one case I worked on, the previous plan was a 400-page monolith that had taken three people six months to write. Of course, it had been published amid great fanfare—and, of course, it had been quickly forgotten. It was not what you would call a useful document.

The One Page Business Plan® takes a thoroughly different approach to planning. Its method prescribes writing a business plan on a single page. The plan itself is designed to be an interactive dynamic document that remains useful throughout the year and the life of the company. Many other business-planning methods use similar thinking but allow more verbiage. One Page holds you to what its name suggests: a single page, simple yet complete, and highly user-friendly.

Consider what a business plan requires in order to be useful:

- **It should be in writing.** This is critical so that the plan can be shared among team members and other stakeholders. The written word has far more power than the spoken: it takes on an authority that discourages argument and has an objective quality that clarifies communication. Putting a plan into writing may be difficult, but doing so is a critical step.

- **It should focus everyone on the planning elements.** A plan should clearly state the vision, mission, objectives, strategies, and action plans that will direct and move you and your team.

- **It should be understandable and versatile.** If the verbiage is complex and not easily understood, the plan loses much of its power. Versatility allows the plan to be adaptable should circumstances change.

The One Page Business Plan® helps you meet all these requirements, as we shall see next.

Using The One Page Business Plan®

When I prepared for my Mount Kilimanjaro expedition, I worked out the One Page plan shown in Figure 2. It provides an example that you can easily transfer to a business situation. This plan clearly delineates what was required for me to reach the summit. It laid out the vision of what I was striving to accomplish as well as my mission, objectives, strategies, and action plans. Because my trip to Africa was a vacation, the plan also laid out other criteria to make it a pleasurable trip, such as visiting the Lutheran missions.

Figure 3 shows a One Page plan for Northwest Electronics, the company I have been using as an example throughout this book. All the components mentioned above are fully delineated in the plan. Let's take a closer look.

Figure 2.
Kilimanjaro: The One Page Business Plan®

Kilimanjaro Expedition
Planning Unit: McQuaig Plan
Fiscal Year: 2005

■ONE
■PAGE
■PLAN

John McQuaig, Climber   Last Updated: 1/1/2006

Stand on the "Roof of Africa."

Vision

Because it's there! Reach a life-long goal of climbing Kilimanjaro.

Mission

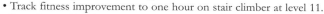

- Track funding for $6,000 budget.
- Track fitness improvement to one hour on stair climber at level 11.
- Recruit two friends to go join the group.
- Hike to the top of Mission Ridge six times prior to the expedition (6200 ft.).

Objectives

- Ensure fitness through a well-researched fitness plan.
- Ensure good health through a well-researched health plan.
- Utilize a well-regarded guide company with experienced guides.
- Develop high-altitude-mountaineering skills through an education program.
- Clearly research and understand the vaccinations available and recommended for Tanzania.
- Combine the trip to Africa with a trip to a couple of missions of the Lutheran Church.

Strategies

- Develop overall plan by 31-JAN-2005.
- Research guide companies and select by 31-MAR-2005.
- Develop budget by 30-APR-2005.
- Develop fitness plan by 30-APR-2005.
- Develop health plan including required inoculations by 31-JUL-2005.
- Launch expedition by 15-JAN-2006.
- Establish plan for photo-taking methods and equipment.
- Read available books on climbing Kilimanjaro.

Action Plans

Figure 3.
Northwest Electronics:
The One Page Business Plan®

Northwest Electronics
Planning Unit: Companywide
Fiscal Year: 2006

:ONE
:PAGE
:PLAN

Jack Terra, CEO   Last Updated: 6/12/20XX

Within the next three years grow Northwest Electronics into a $15 million revenue company providing wholesale electronic products to retail outlets on the West Coast earning a 10% net profit.

Vision

Source and provide successful products!

Mission

Objectives
- Achieve 20XX sales of $11 million.
- Earn pre-tax profits in 20XX of $11 million.
- Reduce the number of Day Sales Outstanding from 75 to 50 by 31-DEC-20XX.
- Increase client satisfaction scores from 7.3 to 8.5 on a 10-point scale.
- Increase market share from 12% to 15%.
- Deliver 95% of product/service orders within three days.
- Decrease order error rates from 5% to 3%.
- Increase internal promotion rate from 35% to 60%.
- Have 95% of vendors achieve 90% of goals.

Strategies
- Focus on upscale urban markets.
- Attract/solicit small business customers needing innovative products.
- Enhance order/shipping execution by using state-of-the-art technology.
- Streamline procurement and vendor processes by limiting to 15 total vendors.
- Expand/improve best practices by understanding industry trends.
- Establish a sales culture through training, shadowing, and mentoring programs.
- Control expenses by using zero-based budgeting.
- Increase shareholder value by stock buyback and limiting dilution.

Action Plans
- Develop a marketing plan by 31-MAR-20XX.
- Complete a potential new market analysis by 31-MAR-20XX.
- Develop a customer satisfaction survey and method to compile by 31-JAN-20XX.
- Develop an employee induction system by 30-JUN-20XX.
- Implement a stock buyback plan by 30-JUN-20XX.
- Develop an employee recruiting plan by 30-JUN-20XX.
- Initiate customer review boards set up by 30-SEP-20XX.
- Complete a systemwide technology review by 30-NOV-20XX.
- Update our best practices annual review by 31-DEC-20XX.

I. The Vision for the Plan

The vision is stated simply and addresses the question "Where do you want the company to be in three to five years?" As you can see, the vision details five important points: the gross revenue ($15 million), the type of products the company will sell (wholesale electronic products), who their customers will be (retail outlets), the geographic extent of the business (West Coast), and net profit (10 percent). This clearly defines where the company will be in three years.

Businesses in different industries have their own particular basic concerns and so create different definitions. I have worked with industries such as banking that define their vision based on asset size and return on assets. I have also worked with industries that, like some service companies, define their business based on the number of full-time employees (FTEs).

Nonprofit organizations can also tailor this approach to their concerns. One vision that we used for a public utility was stated as "Build and lead an innovative organization that delivers long-term benefits to the customer owners of the utility." It clearly expressed that the important elements to them were innovation and benefits to the customer owners. Their charter defined their geographic footprint, so there was no need for them to redefine it. They chose not to limit their business lines because they could see a potential to expand into other areas that could benefit the customer owners.

2. The Mission

In the One Page Business Plan® approach, the mission is the stated reason why the business exists *from the customer's perspective.* This is somewhat different from how other business-planning methods define mission. Because the One Page plan requires that you strictly focus on what benefits exist for the customer, you must put yourself in the customer's shoes before asking, "Why does this company exist?"

FedEx currently defines their mission as "absolutely positively overnight." In their minds, they exist solely to provide customers with overnight delivery. If they fail there, they fail altogether. Since the company began defining their mission in this way, they have completely redesigned their organization, practices, and infra-structure. The result is a highly reliable overnight delivery system with state-of-the-art tracking capabilities.

3. The Objectives

The objectives delineate the results you will measure. What tells you that you are making progress toward your vision? Generally these are stated in terms of the measurable goals for the next year.

As you craft your vision, you will need to establish the measurable objectives that will chart your progress. On a mountain climb, it could include elevation on the mountain and miles of trail covered. In business, it might include sales revenue per month compared to budget and monthly ratings of customer satisfaction scores. In Chapter 8, we look at objectives, including key performance indicators, in great detail.

4. Strategies

Strategies should clearly state how you will accomplish the vision and define how you will go about growing the business. You want to know where you are headed in order to reach the vision. In the case of Northwest Electronics, strategies include focusing on upscale urban markets and attracting small business customers needing innovative products. These define what the company's sweet spot will be relative to who's benefiting from their products.

If you need to emphasize a certain market for strategic purposes, then it's critical that every stakeholder in the organization know what that market is. By way of example, if like Northwest you need to focus on upscale markets, the creation of new upscale developments and communities should interest you in terms of locating potential new customers for your products.

Strategies may also include a certain customer subset, a sales-delivery method, or a set of marketing methods. Northwest Electronics states that one of its strategies is to enhance order/shipping execution by using state-of-the-art technology. For a company like this, it's critical to execute properly on ordering and shipping. There is very little margin for error when a retailer has ordered a particular product from you: the order must not be lost and the correct product must be shipped. Northwest decided that they needed a clear strategy to emphasize the importance of their IT infrastructure in supporting that strategy.

Strategies can also become important when you are determining what your priorities are from the standpoint of an action plan or budgetary allotment. In the case of Northwest, when listing potential outlays for capital expenditure projects, information technology would place near the top of the list because of its importance as a customer-related strategy. Most companies have limited resources, and clear strategic guidance helps them allocate those resources.

5. An Action Plan

The action plan outlines what you will actually do over the next year. In the case of a high-altitude mountain climb, it's important to do such things as get in physical shape, secure appropriate training, and schedule any necessary inoculations if international travel is involved. Northwest Electronics laid out a number of action steps, including the development of a marketing plan. In my experience with small businesses, nothing happens overnight—businesses don't turn on a dime, but make turns one degree at a time. Consequently, if you run a small business, you may need a series of action steps laid out over the course of more than a year.

Business planning has evolved over the years. The typical method of planning calls for a retreat with some soul searching, during which you put together a list of action plans. Typically the company comes out of that retreat with anywhere from 25 to 75 action plans and the full intention to execute them all within the next month. The normal reality is that these plans will be shelved, with very few action steps taken. It is just too difficult to execute in 75 action steps.

The One Page Business Plan® takes a different approach to action planning and lays out the plans in a different manner. First of all, the plans are limited to nine or less. Those nine action plans are then spaced out over the course of the next year so that you have a yearly look at what you are going to do to move the business forward. In addition, this model requires monthly reports on your progress with the plans. There's great power in the simplicity of this method of laying out your action plans. It greatly increases the likelihood that the steps will be executed.

Implementing Your Strategies and Plan

So now that you have developed your strategies and plans, how do you execute them? This is a crucial question because strategy-plan implementation can make the difference between a successful company and a mediocre one. According to Michael Porter (1996, 62), a study of 275 portfolio managers reported that the ability to execute strategy was more important than the quality of the strategy itself. The managers cited strategy implementation as the most significant factor shaping management and corporate valuations.

The One Page Business Plan® is designed for fairly easy implementation, but there are a number of preliminary steps that
management must take for that to happen. These steps include:

- Setting aside time to determine how the plan will be
  implemented
- Looking clearly at who needs to be briefed on the plan and
  how that will be accomplished
- Considering how the change in the organization will be
  managed

Management needs to know the difference between simply surviving
change and mastering it, and has to develop viable change mecha-
nisms to control modifications over the long term. Organizations
don't change: people do. Managers must understand that and ensure
that their people are clear on the need for change and involved in
the implementation effort.

I recently met with management from a company that sells branded
promotional products throughout the United States. Six months
earlier, they had developed a strategic initiative that required
improving their customer relationship management (CRM) process.
After analyzing the available options, they decided to purchase a
relatively expensive CRM software package. They loaded it on their
computer system, trained their sales team to use it, and then rolled it
out. Three months later, they discovered no one was using the
system. Now they wondered how they would go about getting the
salespeople to make the change.

During our discussion of the problem, one of the managers said,
"We need to do what we've always done, and force people to use it.
It's compulsory, not optional!" This is a common response to change
resistance, but it's not a realistic one. As I explained to the managers,
a more productive response would be to work with the sales team

and clarify (1) why it is necessary for them to develop a better understanding of what customers and potential customers are buying and considering buying, and (2) how a CRM system will help them do that. Team members needed to understand that sales are, for the most part, about information management. Once they did, they would be more apt to see the value of the new CRM system and how it would make their jobs easier; consequently, more of them, if not all, would actually use the system.

This suggested approach did not mean that once people began using the system, the wheels of change would swiftly move, free of problems. But at least the implementation effort would be on its way, now strengthened by the team's efforts.

In looking clearly at how a planned change will be managed, you need to consider designing and developing structures for managing the change that are separate from current day-to-day organizational structures. Absent this, the change will just get swallowed up in day-to-day duties and most likely not occur.

Management must also take certain steps as the company rolls out strategic initiatives, including its One Page Business Plan®. Foremost among them is setting aside time for these basic necessities:

- Managing and leading the change effort
- Reviewing the scorecards that come from your key performance indicators on the One Page plan
- Reviewing your action plans and facilitating their ongoing roll-out and implementation

Change and the successful roll-out of strategic initiatives require diligent effort on the part of top management and everyone involved in the organization. Time and resources must be set aside to fulfill this requirement.

It is one thing to dream up a vision and a strategy; it is an entirely different thing to act on them. As analysts report, acting on your strategy is a more important success factor than the quality of the strategy. Although you must take care in developing your strategy and business plan, in the end, if you do not execute that plan, you cannot really be successful. The best plan to climb a mountain will be worthless if you do not actually use it—and climb the mountain.

Chapter Five:
Writing Your Own Story

Many people will tell you their stories of success and failure as you travel up the mountain. Put them out of your mind and write your own story.

—Peter Mata, Kilimanjaro mountain guide
with Recreational Equipment, Inc.

The author on the final summit push on Mt. Kilimanjaro

It was the night before our departure to start climbing Mount Kilimanjaro. After a harrowing ride on a third-world airline into Arusha, Tanzania, I had settled into a very comfortable lodge used mainly by foreigners for wildlife safaris. I knew this would be the last of comfortable nights for quite a while and felt apprehensive about the hostile territory to come.

When the expedition's guide, Peter Mata, held a team briefing, I had a chance to meet my cohorts and discovered I was not the only nervous one. Many of us were second-guessing ourselves, asking questions like, "Did I really prepare adequately? Everyone else seems to be in better shape than I am—can I possibly make the summit?" The latter concern was, of course, paramount: making the summit was the vision for the expedition and abundantly clear to the entire team. On an individual level, nobody wanted to be a member who would break from the team before the vision was realized.

As for our guide, he had a vested interest in the success of each one of us. After safety, the primary key performance indicator for guides and their companies is the percentage of folks they get on the summit. No one wants an unhappy climber, for whom failure is not only a disappointment, but also somewhat of an embarrassment. When the climbers return home, they will be constantly asked if they made the summit. They will want to answer in the affirmative!

Our guide's presentation included stern warnings about the tales we would hear from people coming down the mountain. We would naturally converse with these people, he told us, and the inevitable question of summitting would arise. Along with the answer would come stories of how people got sick from the altitude, couldn't eat the food, got stormed upon, and so forth. They would even include accounts of injuries and perhaps rescues of climbers carried out. The sky was the limit as to what we would hear from people on our way up. And we would have to catalog it as *their* experience and not let it influence ours.

In essence, we had to "write our own story," as Peter put it. He told us not to be concerned about what we heard on the way up: our experience would be different. We should not let the stories of others discourage us, but maintain our focus and determination.

The need for such determination reared its head the next morning a short time before departure. We were at breakfast, seated at a large communal table, when a young woman from Great Britain sat down across from us. She seemed quite fit and up for the challenges of the mountain. But, as we soon learned, she had just come back down, bringing with her some harrowing tales to relate. Her entire team had gotten sick from the altitude, and only a third of them had made it to the summit. That third did not include her. The expedition, she said, was the most miserable experience of her life.

She went on to ask us which route we were taking. We told her we were taking the normal tourist route, or "Coca Cola" route, which goes up a day faster than some of the others. Our answer triggered dire predictions. The woman said she had talked to many people who, having taken that route, later felt tricked because the quicker ascent meant they had less time to acclimatize. In fact, all the climbers she knew who had chosen that route ended up having miserable experiences and few made the summit.

Needless to say, her story and predictions put an immediate damper on our enthusiasm. To renew our spirits, we had to seriously reflect on our guide's advice to "write our own story." In doing so, I told myself, "Well, all that is *her* story or someone else's, not *mine*. Hopefully, mine will be better . . . a lot better!" I wasn't sure it could be a whole lot worse!

Listening as You Write: The Balancing Act

The concept of writing your story relates to many other endeavors in life, including starting a business, running a business, and managing a company department. There will always be other people who have been down the "same" road and are ready with advice. You want to listen to that advice; but remember, you are writing your own story. Don't let the negative thoughts of others bog you down or cause you to abandon your business-building quest altogether. It's a delicate trick to listen as you "write," and to balance learning from others with a determination not to get discouraged if they've had negative experiences.

This balance is easier to achieve if you don't take people's stories too much to heart, but instead try to detect the lessons in them. What productive ideas can you glean from them and apply to your business?

For instance, let's say you're planning to expand your business and happen to talk with someone who used to run a combo bakery and sandwich shop. He hears of your plans and out pours a tale of woe: his business did great the first two years, but when he expanded to a second location, trouble began. It was too difficult to manage both locations properly, and ultimately the business failed because of the expansion and lack of management capability.

Now you can take this story as a stern warning not to expand your business, but to "stick to the knitting" or what has been successful so far. While this may be good advice in some cases, generally the true income potential and opportunity of a business will only be realized through some form of expansion. Thus it is better to ask, "What was wrong in the case of the bakery-sandwich shop owner? Why did he fail? What exactly is the lesson?"

If you review the story, you can see that it was not really the expansion that caused the failure, but rather the owner's inability to manage two locations and properly handle the expansion. Therefore, if you were going to write your own story in this situation, you would want to plan your expansion carefully and ensure that you had the personnel, systems, and management capabilities in place to control the expansion properly.

Working *on* Your Business vs. Working *in* Your Business

Typically, any change to a business, such as expansion, requires the owner to change his or her approach to the business. As small-business consultant Michael Gerber (1995) states in *The E-Myth Revisited: Why Most Small Businesses Don't Work and What to Do About It,* you need to get familiar with the concept of working *on* your business as opposed to working *in* it.

Working on the business involves stepping back from the business and doing some proactive planning and thinking about it. You need to ask yourself:

- If the business were a lump of clay, what would I mold it into? What do I want it to be?
- How can I change the results that I've been getting?
- How do I effect the results in the future and make sure everything is going in the direction I want it to go?

To work on the business, you need to take time out for strategic thinking, the formulation of action plans, and the execution of those plans. This all needs to be done relative to the strategies you have developed.

In our example of the bakery-sandwich shop, when there was a single location, the owner could get by reasonably well by working in the business. He was able to be around most times when the business was open, making sandwiches and baking goods to keep things moving. As the business grew in that location, he hired additional staff, but was still closely involved and able to direct chores. He could quickly step in when problems cropped up or someone called in sick.

As the business expanded and moved to a second location, working in the business became more difficult. He was unprepared for the lack of direct control that he would encounter. In short, he could not be at both shops at the same time. In such a situation, you must properly train the people working at your various locations or quality will start to suffer. Because your attention becomes divided, you cannot closely monitor the quality of all your products. You also can't ensure that customer service is always the best.

Working on your business gives you a much more planned and proactive approach to moving your business forward. It also helps you to clearly identify your goals and vision and how to get there.

Case in Point: Ray Kroc and McDonald's

Gerber's concept of working on the business versus in the business is clearly demonstrated by the case of Ray Kroc and his McDonald's restaurants; the story is well documented and appears in various books about the McDonald's empire.

In the early 1950s, Ray Kroc was selling Multimixer milkshake machines as a salesman throughout the United States. He discovered that two brothers, Dick and Mac McDonald, were using eight machines in their highly systematized restaurant in San Bernardino, California. The brothers had invented the "Speedy Service System," thereby establishing the principle of the modern fast-food restaurant. The brothers had also begun franchising their restaurant concept; however, it was Kroc who recognized the potential for expanding across the country and ultimately around the world.

Generally, whenever Kroc visited a restaurant to pitch his wares, he'd find the owner working furiously—cooking the fries, flipping the burgers, and barking orders at employees. Those orders were always specific instructions on what to do to keep the product quality up and get things done quickly. Kroc's experience with the McDonald brothers' restaurant was different from the start.

There, he found the employees doing the majority of the work while the brothers focused on managing the business. That focus included:

- Reviewing the restaurant's financial operations
- Documenting and creating systems for the employees
- Thinking proactively about how to make things work well within the restaurant and how to improve the operations

Among the brothers' documentation was the "Speedy Service System," which spelled out clearly how the employees were to run the business, including how to cook a hamburger and how to heat the buns.

As Ray Kroc considered buying into various restaurants, he realized that the McDonald brothers' concept could be duplicated. Of course, he never imagined himself actually working in a restaurant, flipping burgers; rather, he envisioned creating a series of these restaurants, ultimately "franchises," where all the systems were clearly documented and everyone was doing the same thing in order to produce the same result. He would be free to work on the business, rather than required to work in it, and could strive at creating value from the business. This radical departure from the approach of other small-restaurant entrepreneurs of the time set him on course for a level of success that, in its enormity, was just as radical.

At the base of it all was McDonald's set of three simple tenets: fast service, consistent quality product, and cleanliness. Around each of these, Kroc established systems to ensure that consistent results would be produced and duplicated everywhere a McDonald's was present. The strength of these systems lay to a great extent in their level of detail, which even included how to heat the hamburger buns. Such detail facilitated the duplication of results across a host of variables, such as regional differences, and, in effect, gave people who bought a McDonald's franchise an education in how to operate and run the business.

These were systems that people were willing to pay for then and, decades later, are still willing to pay for.

Today the business that Kroc created and grew has restaurants in 114 countries and a market capitalization in excess of $40 billion. This is success of legendary proportions—and it all goes back to some very simple considerations, such as proactive thinking, business systemization, and good documentation. In short, it goes back to working *on* the business.

Lessons to Learn

Think about what you do on a daily basis, and then ask yourself:

- How much of my time is spent working in my business?
- How much of my time is spent working on it?

The critical key is to free up time to work on the business. This allows you to "write your own story" as you create your business. Keep in mind that to write that story, you must be aware of how well your business is progressing and moving forward toward your summit. Remember, too, that systematizing your business and creating procedures will free you up to work on the business and still get consistent results from your employees. Above all, learn what you can from others; but don't let their failures dictate your experience.

When Ray Kroc bought into the McDonald's restaurant, he was 52 years old and had diabetes and incipient arthritis. He had lost his gall bladder and most of his thyroid gland. Had he listened to the stories of others, he would have believed he was too old or too sick to succeed. But Kroc said, "I was convinced that the best was ahead of me." Now there's an optimistic writer of stories, and a wise one. He created a business that could work without relying on him doing it all—the only way he could have possibly succeeded in growing beyond one restaurant, let alone thousands.

Chapter Six:
The Team Approach:
Gang Forward!

People acting together as a group can accomplish things which no individual acting alone could ever hope to bring about.

—Franklin D. Roosevelt

The secret is to work less as individuals and more as a team. As a coach I play not my eleven best but my best eleven.

—Knute Rockne

Log: Mount Baker, Northwest Washington, June 1998, 6:30 A.M.

> We have been on Mount Baker for a week participating in a mountain-climbing training seminar run by the American Alpine Institute. Now we are finally approaching the summit, a 10,778-foot snow-capped peak in the Cascade Mountains.

We have been climbing for two hours in a fairly intense blizzard with virtually no visibility. I'm on a rope of three with a mountain guide leading the rope and my 17-year-old son, Logan, on the back.

Progress up the mountain has been slow. At this elevation, each step is followed by a strong, exhaling pressure breath and 10 to 15 seconds of recovery. I'm glad we have an experienced guide who's climbed the mountain many times, because frankly, I can't see much ahead.

Log: Mount Baker, Northwest Washington, June 1998, 7:45 A.M.

I have read about close brushes with the abyss, and now I can write my own humble chapter.

Not long ago, suddenly, without warning, I felt the snow collapse under me and found myself hanging in a crevasse with my feet swinging freely. My backpack had arrested my fall, wedging against the side of the crevasse. I instantly realized there was nothing but air, space, and darkness below me. As I yelled "Falling!" Logan and the guide both dropped into a well-trained self-arrest—a three-point stance that kept me from falling farther in. I was able to reach up, grab the crevasse side, and with adrenaline-fed arms vault myself out of the hole.

The combination of the team, the rope, and my pack kept me from plunging deeper into the crevasse, and I'm safely out of it. Did I say I was glad to have an experienced guide? Now I am grateful to him, my son, my rope—and my backpack.

As my close call on Mount Baker illustrates, teamwork is a critical component of mountaineering. In fact, everything in climbing is designed around this component. Its most basic equipment is a rope—typically 60 meters long and suitable to link three or four climbers—and, under alpine conditions, crampons and ice axes. The quality of this equipment is vital. However, unless climbers know how to use the equipment properly and how to perform well as a team, even the best-made rope or axe will be worthless, if not outright dangerous. For instance, had my teammates on Mount Baker not been trained in executing a three-point stance, they could not have arrested my fall—and my ensuing plunge would also have been theirs, compliments of the rope.

In essence, your life in the mountains is intertwined with those who share your rope. You're only safe to the degree that your teammates and you are capably trained.

Tenzig Norgay, the legendary Sherpa who climbed Mount Everest with Sir Edmund Hillary, learned that lesson early on. In 1934, he was 20 years old and making his first trip to Everest as a porter for a British expedition. The team made it as high as the 22,600-foot pass known as the North Col. At the base of the pass, they came upon a gruesome scene: in a tent shredded by the wind sat the skeletal remains of Maurice Wilson, frozen in the act of putting his boots on. An eccentric Englishman, Wilson had secretly attempted to climb Everest when Tibetan authorities denied him a permit. Because of the secrecy, he hired only three porters, whom he intentionally left below at the base, opting to proceed on his own. With no support or help with deciphering the dire straits he evidently found himself in, Wilson failed to achieve his vision in the worst way possible.

This lone demise taught Norgay a valuable lesson about the importance of teamwork in mountain climbing. It would serve him well almost two decades later, in 1953, during his seventh Everest expedition, this one with a British group led by Colonel John Hunt. Norgay was the trip's *sirdar,* or Sherpa leader, in charge of the Sherpa personnel required to get the expedition to the summit. This was a huge team-building operation, with a corps of members that resembled an army. It included 250 porters whose job was simply to move the two and a half tons of supplies and equipment to the various base camps.

The heart of the expedition team was a group of first-class high-altitude climbers, two of whom the team hoped to get to the summit. Norgay knew that objective, but had no idea if he would have the opportunity to achieve his own vision of reaching the summit. He was willing to accept whatever happened, though. In his own words:

> You do not climb a mountain, like Everest, by trying to race ahead on your own, or by competing with your comrades. You do it slowly and carefully, by unselfish teamwork. Certainly, I wanted to reach the top myself; it was the thing I had dreamed of all my life. But if the lot fell to someone else, I would take it like a man and not a cry baby. For that is the mountain way. (Ullman, 1955, 250)

Tenzig Norgay obviously understood his position as a member of the team. The objective was to get someone on the summit. If he wasn't chosen for the task, he was okay with that. He was a true team player.

As it turned out, the first team from his group to attempt the summit consisted of Tom Bourdillon and Charles Evans. It was only when their valiant effort failed that Tenzig Norgay got his chance to fulfill his dream with Sir Edmund Hillary. Roped together, the pair made their summit bid. Their ascent went safely until, very close to the summit, Hillary lost his footing on a massive chunk of ice and started to fall. As he rapidly slid downward toward certain death, Norgay dug in his ice axe in a three-point self-arrest. Hillary came to a stop. Both were safe! That day, May 29, 1953, Tenzig

Norgay and Edmund Hillary went on to accomplish what many thought impossible: the incredible feat of summitting on Mount Everest.

The teamwork and dedication required to accomplish that feat was monumental. The pair alone could never have succeeded without a strong team to carry the loads to the various camps and to guide their ascent and descent. Absent the team, they could have easily ended up like Maurice Wilson and only reached the North Col before they died.

Is the situation really any different in business? All businesses that have more than one employee or owner consist of teams. Some have one team; some have hundreds or thousands of teams. On a business team, members are tethered together not by a rope but by a common need and desire to fulfill their objective. They are highly reliant on one another for the success or failure of the enterprise or project at hand. Businesses need the power of teams, and teams need the power of each individual member.

Team Power: Strength and Feedback

The main force of any team is found in its ability to provide two essentials:

1. Strength in carrying out the mission at hand
2. Feedback within its membership and to the leaders or managers at the mission's ultimate helm

When you're climbing a mountain, team strength provides a measure of safety, via the rope, that otherwise would not exist; it also provides physical strength to share the load.

Feedback is also a vital element of teamwork. One of the biggest risks in high-altitude mountain climbing is acute mountain sickness (AMS). This potentially fatal illness results from improper acclimatization to your elevation, and includes the symptoms of appetite loss, fatigue, dizziness, and disorientation. The latter is especially dangerous as it diminishes your understanding of your condition: classically, climbers developing AMS cannot "connect all the dots" to realize what is happening to them. Lack of oxygen and the intense desire to summit only contribute to this blinding. In such a situation, teammates are crucial. With members on the alert for hazards like this and focused on the moment, the climb to the summit is safer, and the summit more attainable on a collective team level.

A business team needs its members to provide feedback to each other so that the hazards of business can be avoided. One member may see the big risks that are out there, while the leadership may not. A well-oiled team will digest feedback and adjust its course.

There's a lot of strength in a business team that can be organized and utilized much like a mountain-climbing team. The members of the business team need to recognize that they are "roped together." Their successes and failures proceed from a common mission. If they work it right, they can capitalize on that common goal. If a team has a clearly articulated goal with objectives that lead it to the goal, its members are more apt to become a powerful force in accomplishing that goal.

The Critical Factor: Managing for High Performance

The amount of strength and quality of feedback provided by a team is dependent on the team's ability to work well as a cohesive unit. For mountaineering teams, this kind of high performance is a matter of survival. The situation is similar in business, where low-performing groups can undermine an entire organization. It's thus critical that teams be properly managed and their strengths capitalized upon.

Managing or coaching teams for high performance is an art onto itself. A good example of management's own power in this area is the successful turnaround that CEO Gordon Bethune and his team achieved for Continental Airlines. On the jacket of his book, *From Worst to First,* Bethune summarizes and describes the status of the organization when he assumed leadership in 1994:

> It was a company coming apart at the seams. Running at a loss of nearly $55 million a month and unable to pay its bills, Continental was on the verge of filing for bankruptcy for the third time in a decade. . . . In terms of quality, Continental was rated the worst across the board and by a wide margin, among the nation's biggest ten airlines. Employee morale was at rock bottom. Underpaid and embittered over having to take the rap for ineffective revolving-door management, many of the rank-and-file actually ripped the company logos off their uniforms. (1998)

Within months of taking the helm at Continental, Bethune and his new team were able to completely reverse direction. Bethune ascribes the major thrust of this reversal to a radical change in the company's team dynamics. That change was facilitated by the adoption of three key performance indicators that were tracked in real time: on-time arrivals, lost luggage, and customer complaints.

The CEO's account of one of his regularly scheduled meetings with employees gives us some insight into his idea of teamwork. The subject was employee bonuses that management had set up based upon on-time aircraft. Everyone in the organization was eligible to receive those rewards, prompting one worker to ask: "I can understand that for the baggage handlers, pilots, and others directly involved in the process, but why are people like reservation agents getting bonuses?" Bethune replied that the situation was like his watch. Every part of the watch was doing a job that ultimately resulted in an accurate timepiece. Which part of the watch should he get rid of? Which part would not deserve a bonus for the work it was doing?

Bethune's team vision brought about a complete cultural shift within the company. Many disgruntled employees with fractured relationships among themselves and with management ultimately achieved the seemingly impossible: they scaled an Everest of problems to develop into a cohesive team. Their motivation? Key performance indicators that, in their limited number, were comprehensible and brought the true team concept to the forefront. Bethune credits the team concept and development as the most important element in lifting Continental from its worst-airline status to its 1997 designation as "Airline of the Year" by *Transport World*.

Of course, in both mountaineering and business, a well-managed team is a stronger team, with a significant increase in the likelihood of success. Let us now consider how to build and manage a strong team.

The Requirements of High Performance

In managing teams, you must keep in mind that the all-important factor of high performance comes with its demands. To reach a true "summit" of performance, teams require all of the following:

- A shared mission or purpose that motivates or inspires members
- Autonomy and authority for the tasks they must perform
- Interdependence and shared leadership
- Broadly defined jobs and responsibilities
- Meaningful participation in decision making

Teams should achieve higher performance than individuals working solo, with the sum of the collective greater than that of the individual parts. In essence, a high-performance team should be a self-managing, multifunctional group of people organized around a goal and empowered with full responsibility for their success.

The Elements of a Team Model

There are three elements of a team model:

1. **Charter.** The charter for a team should include the team's purpose, goals, vision, and a list of its internal and external customers. For example, the team's vision for a climbing expedition would have everyone on the summit, and its goals would include a safe and injury-free expedition. For a business sales team, the goal might be sales of $1 million per month with a gross margin of 30 percent.

2. **Design.** The design for the team includes what core work processes may be involved, how roles and responsibilities will be shared or delineated, the procedures and norms that will be followed, and the systems that need to be in place for the team to function properly.

3. **Relationships.** The relationships for the team include the level of trust and respect that will exist within the team, how communication will flow, what sort of cohesion there will be, and what synergy will be involved.

The team-model elements are interdependent, but their development generally requires the sequence shown above. For instance, you need to start with a vision for the team; then the other elements, such as communication, procedures, norms, and systems can be aligned with achieving that vision.

Think about the teams you've been involved with. How clearly have the elements of the team model been defined?

Team Types

High-performance teams share a number of common characteristics, but generally they can be classified as one of the four team types shown below.

Examples of Team Types

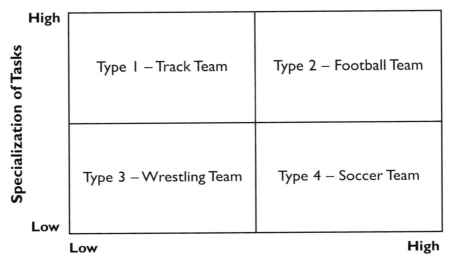

Coordination Between Team Members

Type 1 teams have a high level of specialization, with specialty skills that vary with each team member or team subgroup. The work is divided among the various specialties, with very little coordination between them. For instance, on a track team, you have field events as well as track events. The 280-pound shot putter doesn't have much in common with the 170-pound 100-yard dash sprinter. Moreover, the success of the shot putter is not dependent on the speed that the 100-yard dash is run. Yet the two athletes are bound together on a team whose success is interdependent at the team level. They can be stars in their own individual right—in fact, in Type 1 teams, individual results are usually prized more than team results. Still, any team success relies on the whole team.

Type 2 teams are composed of people from different types of disciplines, but require a higher degree of coordination than Type 1 teams. For example, on a football team, you can have the best quarterback in the world, but if the receivers lack the talent to get downfield and into the open and actually catch the ball, the team's not going to win many games. Success requires coordination between all 11 players.

Type 3 teams, like wrestling teams, are low in specialization and coordination. All the wrestlers basically do the same thing; they just come in a variety of sizes and occupy different weight classes. The coordination is not important because each of them is on the mat at a different time: what happens in the 119-pound class has no effect on what occurs in the heavyweight class. The ultimate team score is based on the compilation of the members' individual results.

Type 4 teams basically do the same thing. For instance, in soccer, players need to kick and dribble the ball as well as pass it, and require high coordination. If you watch a winning soccer team, you'll soon realize why it's successful: each member is skilled at passing the ball and advancing it to where someone gets a shot at the goal. The team is also able to coordinate defensive efforts to avoid getting scored against.

Type 4 teams are generally organized around completing a whole task, but their members are also cross-trained to do one another's jobs. Each of them could potentially move into another position on the team and do reasonably well. They wouldn't be fully trained as a defenseman or winger, but a forward could pinch-hit in those positions. Obviously, success here resides at the team level. Fans might watch the star forward who scores often, but everyone cares most about the team results.

Think again about the teams you've been involved with. With what type of team have you worked most often? If you have worked with a variety of team types, which team type met with the greatest success?

Team Building: The Four Stages of Team Development

For us to understand how a high-performance team is built and managed, it is useful to consider the enduring work of psychologist B. W. Tuckman. In 1965, he clearly identified the stages of development necessary to build a team into an effectively productive unit. There are four stages in all:

1. Forming   3. Norming
2. Storming   4. Performing

Over time, Tuckman's work on these stages has seasoned well and is no less useful to business leaders today than when it was first advanced. Let's take a closer look at Tuckman's explanation of these stages.

1. Forming

During this first stage, steps are taken to assemble the group, which at this point is simply a collection of individuals. In the forming stage, the group's purpose or vision is discussed along with its title, intended lifespan, composition, and leadership. Consensus, to some degree, is usually reached. Individuals work at establishing their personal identities in the group and make some impression on the others.

Here, people typically start out with a lack of direction and unity, and seek both as relationships begin to develop. This behavior was evident in our Kilimanjaro team during our first get together. Once we met one another, relationships started to form and communication lines started to develop.

2. Storming

According to Tuckman (1965), this is where the group attempts to work together. Storming is generally an accurate description of this stage, as the group's initial consensus often fragments and some measure of frustration and disharmony develops. It's a difficult stage for a team. Members begin to realize the amount of work that lies ahead of them. They start to understand some of the strengths and weaknesses of their teammates, and irritability may result from that.

In the storming process, people may argue about the future of the team, its goals, and how to put it together. Various leaders may try to rise to the top and sub-groups may develop, trying to exert power within the team. Members have not yet worked out their roles, and are inexperienced enough with one another that interpersonal clashes may result.

However tough this stage can be, it's essential to team building. If properly handled, storming leads to the formation of more realistic objectives, procedures, and norms. Members also learn a great deal more about one another.

3. Norming

The norming stage is where members are finally able to reconcile and establish some direction around their relationships. They become more function oriented and are able to work on roles and responsibilities. Here the team's vision and goals become clearer. Normally, conflict lessens as people start to accept the limitations and weaknesses of others and allow a more natural process of development to occur.

The team, at this point, is able to experience some stability. Its processes and systems as well as interrelationships develop further, providing members with a means of moving toward the team vision.

4. Performing

Only when the previous three stages have been completed will the team reach the optimum performance level, the performing stage. This is where the full power and effectiveness of the team comes to the forefront. Now the challenge is to keep the team at this stage.

Normally, performing does not remain completely consistent. A performing team may suffer changes that cause it to slip into bad habits. Members need to stay clearly focused on the team vision and correct any rising disharmony. Quite often, by changing procedures or communication lines, the team can be put back on a performing basis.

A basic understanding of these team-development stages and the other topics that have been presented in this chapter should help you build stronger teams and manage them for high performance.

Keep in mind that a business team, like a mountaineering team, can encounter crevasses and unstable ground in its quest to meet its goals. In such a situation, the kind of teamwork and dedication exemplified by Tenzig Norgay is just as applicable to business as to mountaineering. Help the members of your teams reach these heights through an approach to leadership and coaching that, like Gordon Bethune's, acknowledges the value of teams and their important contribution to strengthening the entire organization.

Chapter Seven:
Finding a Sherpa
Who Knows the Trail

I absolutely believe that people, unless coached, never reach their maximum potential.

—Bob Nardelli, CEO, Home Depot

When you enter the mountains with the intention of climbing the summit, you enter an extremely dangerous zone. I've seen the temperatures drop by 50 degrees in 10 minutes. I've watched the heat of day open up crevasses and change the glaciers under them. I've even fallen into a crevasse myself. Dangers lurk very nearby. In such an environment, one of the most critical necessities for keeping safe and achieving success is a Sherpa—an experienced guide.

Peter Mata, our "Sherpa" on Mount Kilimanjaro, is a perfect example of such a guide. He had summitted Kilimanjaro over 600 times prior to our climb and knew every nuance of the mountain, including its weather, trail conditions, and snow conditions. In addition, he had worked with thousands of individuals trying to achieve the summit goal and knew the best way to help make that happen. His experience had taught him when to push and when to back off, and how to factor in potential problems with fatigue and illnesses like altitude sickness. He and his team were the principal reason we succeeded in reaching the summit.

The first major mountain I climbed was Mount Rainier in the Cascade Range in Washington State. At 14,400 feet, it stands out like a beacon and is visible from most of the state's western region. When I first considered the endeavor, I had no prior experience in mountaineering. I researched the possible guide services and discovered that Rainier Mountaineering, Inc. (RMI) had the exclusive guide contract for the mountain at that time. They offered a one-day mountaineering training class, which included learning self-arrest, rest step, and pressure breathing. Once through that, and if approved by the instructors, I would be able to attempt the mountain on a two-day summit expedition. I was game.

Once my training was finished, with approval received, I went on to the climb. Our group of 14 people was assigned four guides: the most experienced had reached the summit over 200 times; the least-experienced, over 50 times. They knew the mountain very well. They also knew how our bodies would react and what might happen to us as we moved to a higher elevation. Without this group of dedicated professionals, I would have never tried to climb that mountain: I would have lacked many of the skills necessary for safety and success.

As you enter business, you also enter into a dangerous environment. There may not be literal crevasses, but there are plenty of figurative ones. The statistics tell us that 80 percent of small businesses fail in the first five years—a daunting percentage that you don't want to fall into. However, with a mentor, guide, or coach to assist you in developing and growing your business, the risk of failure radically decreases, because you have secured one of the more crucial keys to the summit of business success.

The Power of Business Coaching

Coaching is a leading tool that savvy business people use to develop extraordinary businesses. Through periodic coaching sessions, clients clearly identify what's most important to them and learn to structure their thoughts, words, and actions in a way that propels them toward their vision. In general, coaching provides unparalleled help in three important areas:

1. **Vision and Goals:** Determining what you truly want to accomplish, both personally and professionally

2. **Progress Monitoring:** Keeping track of, and reviewing, your current course of action to ensure it is productive and will lead to the desired results

3. **Support:** Obtaining the tools, structure, and other assistance you need in order to accomplish what you want—and more

1. Vision and Goals

A good coach will help you determine precisely what you want to achieve not only in your professional life but in your personal life as well. For most entrepreneurs, it's important to align personal and business goals because, otherwise, problems can develop down the line. For example, suppose you want to grow your business at 30 percent a year and calculate that this goal will require you to work 60 hours per week. While that workload may be fine on a professional level, it may impede your lifestyle goals, with negative consequences for your family. With your coach's help, you will be able to recognize this potential conflict.

In a situation such as this, in which present or potential conflicts are detected, the coach will ask probing questions designed to help you analyze your motivation. For instance, do you want a 30 percent sales increase for sound business reasons, or because your ego is pushing you to stay ahead of some nasty competitor? Quite often, we entrepreneurs jump into business moves without clearly thinking through what we're doing and why we're doing it. A good coach makes you aware of such impulses, requiring you to review your goals and clarify them so that you understand what you're actually trying to accomplish.

2. Progress Monitoring

Coaching also prompts you to review the actions you're taking to ensure that you produce results as quickly and as judiciously as possible. When you have someone assisting you with monitoring your progress toward your vision, you're in a better position to recognize process slowdowns. And should slowdowns occur, your coach will know the questions to raise about what's derailing your process, thus helping you speed up the assessment and redirection process.

3. Support

Finally, the coach will help you get the tools, structure, and other support you need to accomplish more. Part of the coach's job is to be familiar with the issues that may develop and confront your business, and to know what types of resources are available to you. Coaches are in a position to direct your efforts and help you find solutions to your hurdles.

The Need for Coaching: An Example

Over the years, I've known many entrepreneurs who were strong in their main business area, but weak in marketing and sales. Typically, they had been trained in a certain discipline and were comfortable exercising it, but not selling it. For instance, I worked with a surveyor who was highly skilled at surveying and analyzing property and judging the potential for property; however, he felt uncomfortable selling surveying services. He also had virtually no marketing or sales training. As a result, the marketing and sales portion of his business suffered.

In coaching someone like this, the first step is to create a marketing and sales plan for how the practice will be presented and grown to new customers. In terms of the surveyor, because I had seen this type of situation in a number of business environments and had extensive experience helping businesspeople create marketing plans, I could offer solid coaching assistance. I was also familiar with a number of software tools, customer-relationship management tools, and other programs that could address his weaknesses. As a result, I was able to direct him to the appropriate tools for succeeding in his sales effort.

Staying Clear on the Coach's Job

Keep in mind that coaching is not psychological therapy. Therapists help clients examine their pasts to deal with any number of personal problems. Therapy aims to "fix" psyches; business coaching aims to fix businesses. Coaching—whether in mountaineering or business—is an action-oriented process focused primarily on the present and future.

A coach's job is to ask the right questions and help clients analyze where they are now and how they can continue to move toward their vision. To do the job well, the coach must consider three basic questions:

1. **Who?** Who is the business owner who needs coaching, and what are his or her personal needs and business vision? What defines success for this individual? What does he or she hope to get out of the business?
2. **How?** How will the vision be achieved? What strategies are necessary? How can they be aligned with personal goals?
3. **What?** What are the precise goals that the person wants to achieve in the business?

Coaches enable clients to provide the answers through the work done in the coaching relationship. The result is that clients have an expert who will help them with the design and implementation of their business endeavor, and with whom they can later share the success or failure of that endeavor.

Company-Based Employee Coaching

Many companies have discovered the benefit of offering company-wide coaching to employees. Generally, they don't try to force this on the employees, but rather have it available as a resource for employee development. What typically happens is the company hires one or two consultants who are available to work with employees on an as-needed basis. An employee may have recently been moved to a supervisory position and need assistance in transferring his or her skills to the new manager environment; or there may be a particular issue that needs to be worked through in a department and an individual coach meeting with each of the employees could help the department move through the issue.

One company that has reported a significant benefit from employee coaching is Metropolitan Life Insurance Company. MetLife hired a consulting firm to provide coaching to their retail sales force. Based on the independent coaching and assistance, their productivity increased by an average of 35 percent, while 50 percent identified new markets to develop. MetLife also found that their retention rates increased and that all of the employees were retained throughout the coaching process. Typically, the insurance sales business has a fairly high turnover rate, so this was a major improvement. MetLife also reported that although the coaching program cost $620,000, it delivered $3.2 million in measurable gains. That is a considerable return on investment.

Accepting the Need for Coaching

Coaching for many people is a lifelong process. Consider Tiger Woods. He became the greatest golfer in the world based on highly specific coaching at a very young age. Despite his amazing skills, even today he continues to depend on a coach for help and training on a regular basis.

Why do we sometimes think we can do things without assistance and without coaching, when one of the best performers in the world still finds a need for a coach every day?

Businesses regularly use coaches to help move their people forward. Why? Because they get results and advance toward their goals. As an entrepreneur, you must realize it will be difficult to make progress toward *your* goals without some element of coaching. Find someone who knows your "territory"—who has been down this trail before, assisting other people in achieving their goals—and enlist that person in helping you achieve your goals.

Chapter Eight:
How Do You Eat an Elephant?

Answer to the above: *One bite at a time.*

> —Traditional American joke

Every company, every boardroom in which I sit, has a plan, and they have objectives, goals, and a process.

> —Vernon Jordan

There's been a consistency of approach and a consistency of execution. Moving to a common system and common metrics has really helped us.

> —Rick Wagoner

To anybody other than a pack of hungry lions, eating an elephant would seem a daunting task. It's a monumental amount of meat to consume. How would you actually do it? One bite at a time. Everything that gets accomplished in life is accomplished one step, or one bite, at a time.

When you climb mountains, you can't get discouraged by the distance to the summit. You've got to take comfort in the knowledge that it can be done one step at a time.

Most of the mountains I've climbed are volcanoes sitting high above the landscape surrounding them. When approaching mountains like that, you realize how incredibly high they are compared to anything else in sight. If you focus too much on the end destination, it's easy to get discouraged.

Often it's more encouraging to watch your key indicators as you progress toward the summit. If you began your climb to a 14,000-foot summit at 4,000 feet, it's a relief when you know that you've reached the 9,500-foot mark. This type of benchmark allows you to chart your progress. As I climb a mountain, I concentrate on how much altitude I have already accomplished rather than how much more there remains for me to climb. If the trail is a continual ascent, you know that for every thousand feet you manage to scale, you've gotten that much closer to the summit.

Obviously, to track your progress toward a goal, you need a vision of where you're headed (for more on vision, see Chapter 2). Once that is defined, you must ask, "What key performance indicators (KPIs)—or metrics, or objectives—will indicate that you're making progress toward that vision?" In this context, *key performance indicators, metrics,* and *objectives* are generally interchangeable terms, meaning *quantifiable units of measurement.* I will use the term *KPI.*

What You Can Measure, You Can Manage

The title for this section is an excellent business mantra. Unless you have a means of measuring an activity, process, or result, you have no effective way of managing it. Your only source of feedback is a gut feeling and not necessarily reliable. In order to properly manage an activity, you first need to figure out how to measure it.

Measurements usually fall into three specific categories:

1. **Activity measurement.** This is a straight measurement of activity. For example: 1,500 units of product A were produced this week; six new employees were hired in the marketing division; 16 cold calls were logged this week.

2. **Results comparison.** Compares one period's results against another period's results. For example: gross sales were up 12 percent this month compared to last year; administrative expenses were down 3 percent related to the prior year.

3. **Business performance.** Compares actual business performance against a goal such as the sales volume we projected this month versus actual sales.

There are a number of critical factors that determine the KPIs' level of value and effectiveness. These need to be taken into account as you design the indicators for your business. Bearing in mind that the main purpose of KPIs is to predict the future course of the business, we need to look to the economic realm to find some additional ways to filter the measurements.

Indicators in the Economic Realm

Simon Kuznets (1901–1985) was a Russian-raised Nobel Prize winner and Harvard economics professor. He studied the various types of indicators and how they related to predicting economic behavior. He found that the indicators fell into three classifications depending on their time frames:

1. **Leading indicators,** which anticipate business cycles and the direction of the economy

2. **Coincident indicators,** which synchronize with the business cycles and provide information about the current state of the economy

3. **Lagging indicators,** which follow changes in business cycles and tell the historical story of the economy

These classifications are used by the Conference Board, popularly known for its Consumer Confidence Index, to track economic activity and produce data on where the economy is headed. To better understand the differences between the indicators, consider the following examples, which specify what the Board tracks.

Leading Indicators (Anticipate business cycle)
- Average workweek
- Initial unemployment claims
- New orders for consumer goods and materials
- Plant and equipment orders
- New building permits for private housing units
- M1 and M2 money supply
- Plant and equipment orders

Coincident Indicators (In sync with business cycle)
- Number of employees on non-agricultural payroll
- Industrial production
- Manufacturing and trade sales volume
- Civilian employment to population ratio
- Gross Domestic Product

Lagging Indicators (Follow changes in business cycle)
- Average duration of employment
- Manufacturing and trade inventories
- Commercial loans
- Ratio of consumer debt to personal income
- Short-term interest rates

This list not only clarifies the differences between the types of indicators, but also suggests the indicators' relative importance in predicting the economy's future behavior. For example, the leading indicator of "new building permits for private housing units" provides a much clearer suggestion of future activity in the economy's construction sector than the lagging indicator of short-term interest rates. When combined with several additional measures, the list gives economists a reasonable (though imperfect) prediction of where the economy is going and a fairly clear picture of where it has been.

Translation to Business

How does this approach translate to the small-business environment? With the exception of coincident indicators, which are not typically used in business, it translates quite well. Leading indicators, which help predict what will happen in the future, are especially important. For example, in sales, you might include as a leading indicator the number of initial contacts your salespeople are making. You can generally chart a correlation between these contacts and your sales results four months down the line. An additional indicator would be the number of incoming calls on your order line. Leading indicators like this are very useful as tracking devices because of their reasonably high level of predictability.

In business, lagging indicators are helpful as historical records. An example would be a key performance indicator such as "actual sales for the month of September." It tells you what your sales were for September, although, obviously, it does not tell you what the sales may be in October, November, and December. Lagging indicators are particularly useful for comparing recent activity to that of previous years; but they are not as meaningful for a business as leading indicators.

When you design the KPIs for your business, you want to rely on good balance between leading and lagging indicators, with a stronger emphasis on leading indicators.

Keep in mind that you can be creative with these indicators. I recently met with a manager of a restaurant chain and we discussed the KPIs used by his business. He said the most useful KPI came by way of mystery-shopper surveys. Such surveys are conducted by firms for hire to test your customer service and quality of service. A consultant will shop anonymously at your establishment or dine at your restaurant, and report back with a scorecard on the business. In the case of a restaurant, grades are given for friendliness of service, speed of service, quality of the food, and any other factor integral to the quality of the dining experience. The grades are then averaged into a numerical rating.

The manager with whom I met explained that his company schedules surveys three times a month. The overall rating is the number one indicator of the level of sales to expect over the next three months at the location tested. As a bonus, the mystery-shopper surveys also keep his team of employees focused on the service and quality of experience they are providing.

KPIs and Their Role in Continental's Comeback

In Chapter 6, we saw how Gordon Bethune's team approach helped to reverse the impending demise of Continental Airlines in the mid 1990s. In chronicling the air carrier's recovery and its subsequent rise to first place in the airline industry, Bethune (1998) also underscores the crucial role played by measurement—in particular, the tracking of three leading KPIs: on-time arrival, lost luggage, and customer complaints.

When Bethune's team initiated their work, Continental ranked dead last in all three indicators. Interestingly enough, these indicators were already being tracked by the Department of Transportation: they were neither complicated nor novel. However, although Bethune did not dream them up, he did realize they needed to be emphasized.

In Bethune's analysis, the airlines had been too controlled by accountants and overly focused on cost per available mile. Although that is a standard KPI for airlines and measured by all, in Continental's case, product was suffering as a result. Bethune had his war cry: We aren't in business to make money; we're in business to put out a good product. "You can make a pizza so cheap nobody wants to eat it," he said, "and you can make an airline so cheap that nobody wants to fly it" (1998, 50). There's a huge difference between cost control and stinginess: in general, companies must consider the effects of their investments on the customer and then maximize the utilization of their funds.

Once Bethune had his analysis, he turned around the nature of the company's indicators from lagging to leading. Rather than worrying too much about cutting costs, he focused the company on what was important to customers. First, he asked those customers what was critical, and used their responses for his three main KPIs—on-time arrival, lost luggage, and customer complaints. These were leading indicators because they told him whether or not customers would fly with Continental again.

Next, Bethune had the company start tracking the KPIs in real time. Employees rallied, now feeling they were part of a genuine team with a valuable goal. They even set up scoreboards in luggage areas and breakrooms to see how they were doing on the indicators. This effort refocused the company, which went on to find innovative ways to get planes to their destinations on time and to avoid lost luggage. They designed systems and changed processes to improve performance in all these areas.

We can learn a great deal from Bethune's experience and approach. He reinvented his airline, Continental, and focused his team on precisely what his customers cared about the most. What things do your customers *really* care about? How can you measure success in achieving them?

The Balanced Scorecard

When designing KPIs for a company or department, you may want to consider using an additional measurement filter: the balanced scorecard. This approach was initiated and developed by Harvard business professors Robert S. Kaplan and David P. Norton, and first presented in their 1996 book, *Balanced Scorecard*. A series of books on the concept later followed.

The work of Kaplan and Norton was a response to the purely financial scorecards that many companies were judged on. These theorists felt that companies needed a more comprehensive approach that would include more leading indicators and provide more balance to the many functional areas of an organization. Kaplan and Norton put it this way:

> The balanced scorecard retains traditional financial measures. The financial measures tell the story of past events, an adequate story for industrial-aged companies for which investments, long-term capabilities, and customer relation-ships are not critical for success. These financial measures are inadequate, however, for guiding and evaluating the journey that information-aged companies must make to create future value through investment and customers, suppliers, employees, processes, technology, and innovation. (1996, 7)

In this context, a company may be doing well on financial goals, but may not be sustainable because learning and growth have not been propagated within the company. Kaplan and Norton's preferred "balanced scorecard" is designed to address the problem through four components:

1. Learning and growth perspective
2. Business process perspective
3. Customer perspective
4. Financial perspective

1. Learning and Growth Perspective

This scorecard component focuses on how you are developing your employee base. It looks at employee training and corporate cultural attitudes related to both individual and corporate self-improvement. The development of employee and corporate knowledge is a critical element here, given the shift toward a knowledge-based economy. Also, because of the increased reliance on knowledge workers in many organizations, and the extreme reliance on these workers in knowledge-based companies, organizational stakeholders need to understand how learning and growth are being managed.

In the knowledge-based organization, the knowledge worker is the company's only repository of true intelligence. Because such companies' main resources are knowledge and work, they must measure their investment in learning and growth to adequately project future sustainability.

Many companies that have a knowledge-based workforce have difficulty finding new employees who fit their technical needs. If they are not training their existing employees, a "brain drain" will ensue. The learning and growth perspective, if properly designed, should measure the strength of the "brain trust" and how it is developing in the organization.

Kaplan and Norton also emphasize that learning is more than just training. They look beyond normal training metrics and consider indicators like mentors and tutors within the organization. Also important is the degree of ease in communication among workers, which should allow quick information exchange to solve problems. Other indicators may include the technological tools that are being developed within the company. In short, learning and growth indicators include all the items that increase the organization's technological intelligence.

2. Business Process Perspective

This scorecard component looks at the development of internal business processes. It measures KPIs such as process development and documentation. For a company to have ongoing sustainability, it needs clearly defined and efficient processes for handling all its various tasks.

Developing and documenting specific business processes is vital for all organizations, yet smaller companies are usually not good at it. This is a problem that also attracted the attention of Michael Gerber (1995) in *The E-Myth Revisited*. Gerber states that a critical issue for small businesses is the tendency of the owner or a small number of managers to maintain all the intellectual intelligence for the organization. They alone know how to handle the company's major business processes, production flow, sales, billing, and marketing. This reliance on a small number of people puts the organization at risk and is one of the primary reasons that it's difficult to sell or transition a business to new owners.

Gerber goes on to posit that the only way true value can be grown within a business is by decreasing the reliance on the entrepreneur and increasing the reliance on systems that are in place. In order for systems to be effective, they need to be documented.

3. Customer Perspective

Kaplan and Norton's third scorecard component recognizes the high importance of the customer. Management philosophy has recently increased its emphasis on understanding the customer perspective in business, finding that a strong customer focus is essential for a business to succeed.

In his book, *Who Says Elephants Can't Dance?*, Louis V. Gerstner, Jr. (2002) describes what he inherited when he took over as IBM's CEO in 1993. New to the struggling organization, he discovered a strong internal focus at IBM, but no customer focus. In fact, its culture so hampered customer focus and innovation that it had virtually eliminated them. In many cases, innovative products developed within the company were taken outside it and brought to market much faster. Gerstner's management team needed to find a way to make IBM more nimble and responsive to the needs of the marketplace, and to work together to reestablish IBM's mission as a customer-focused provider of computer solutions. This effort, led by Gerstner, was successful to a large degree, thus transforming the company and representing a major turnaround for it.

To become customer focused and stay that way, companies must continually survey customer satisfaction and find ways to improve their processes, products, and services based on customer feedback. Kaplan and Norton recommend that the results of customer surveys, such as mystery shopping, be tracked within the customer perspective, since they are the leading indicators of future sales. The importance of such testing cannot be stressed enough, because if customers are not satisfied, they will eventually find other suppliers to meet their needs.

4. Financial Perspective

Prior to the development of the balanced scorecard, this perspective was really the only one that mattered. Kaplan and Norton continued to recognize its importance, but put it on equal footing with their other three perspectives. The focus here is on adequate working capital and sustainable profitability. These are the organizational elements tested in the financial area and include many of the various financial ratios, such as the current ratio and return on equity.

The Scorecard in Practice

The theory behind the balanced scorecard is that entrepreneurs and business leaders must look at all four of these perspectives and not allow one to take precedence over the others and be assigned more weight. However, from time to time, a company may need to tilt the balance temporarily, emphasizing one or more perspectives over the others or deemphasizing a perspective. For instance, a company may decide to put less emphasis on the learning perspective as they try to return to profitability and work harder on the financial perspective. In the long run, they won't be able to sustain themselves if they aren't learning and growing, but for short periods of time, they might be okay with deemphasizing one perspective.

As you develop your own scorecard, you need to consider whether your KPIs are leading, coincident, or lagging. An emphasis on leading indicators will give you a perspective on the future direction and results of the company. You should also filter your KPIs based on the balanced scorecard approach, with a fairly equal number of KPIs in each of the four areas of the scorecard.

Determining the Optimum Number of Measurements

Clients often ask me, "How many KPIs should a company be tracking and how often?" With the proliferation of computer data and the ability to sort data in many ways, it's fairly common to see complex and lengthy scorecards with up to 50 different measurements being tracked. Judging from my experience, that's far too many to expect a management team to handle. In general, I suggest no more than nine measurements for the overall company KPIs and no more than nine measurements per department. If that seems like too few, consider that Gordon Bethune was able to completely reinvent Continental Airlines using only three high-level KPIs.

To determine your KPIs, you must look clearly at your company or organization and ask, "What are the indicators that matter to our customers and that will help us transform our company?" Track those; then look at the more detailed KPIs "underneath" that might drive those top indicators.

For instance, in Bethune's example, it was important to track lost luggage companywide. I'm sure there were KPIs reported underneath that, which tracked the number of lost luggage in more detailed metrics for the luggage-handling department. Specifics in this area might include sick days for employees, since a lot of breakdowns occur when people are off work and replacement employees are brought in. They might also include a learning and growth perspective of processes and systems within the luggage-handling department. There can be a number of detailed scorecards housed under the umbrella of the companywide scorecards.

If you have too many KPIs, the company will stray toward micro management. Senior management will feel it necessary to tell their department heads how to do their job based on the detailed KPIs being measured. Clearly, this is not desirable. A well-designed high-level scorecard system sets the big-picture measurement for what matters to the customer and the growth of the organization. The individual departments and managers should then develop their own reporting systems. They will need to track for themselves the more detailed key performance indicators that will show their contribution to the overall goals.

Taking It One Step at a Time

I have learned from years of both mountaineering and business management that nothing happens instantly. You need to take on the mountain one step at a time. You need to make changes in business one step at a time.

Tracking the progress toward your "summits" is critical to managing your "summit" bid and keeping everyone informed. Measuring your progress will greatly increase the probability of success.

Chapter Nine:
The Dilemma of Luck

Luck is a dividend of sweat. The more you sweat, the luckier you get.

—Ray Kroc

The harder I work, the luckier I get.

—Samuel Goldwyn

The final key to the summit is simply luck. You can clearly set your expectations and follow all the steps to success that experienced climbers have outlined, including how to deal with your weaknesses; but in the end, luck will not be denied. It will have the final say in the outcome.

In his bestselling book, *Into Thin Air,* Jon Krakauer (1997) describes his now famous climb on Mount Everest. On May 10, 1996, in clear weather, he and his expedition team set off on the final stretch of their bid for the summit. Krakauer reached the mountain's pinnacle in the early afternoon; then, after spending several minutes there, he began his long descent. Meanwhile, other members of his team were still pushing on toward the summit. Around Everest, gathering clouds now obscured Pumori, Ama Dablam, and other lesser peaks. Little did Krakauer or his teammates know that a deadly freak storm was sweeping up the mountain. By the time he reached his base camp, the storm had claimed the lives of nine climbers from four expedition teams, including his own team. It was the most devastating day ever on Everest.

As Krakauer's experience illustrates, you simply cannot foresee every event or development that will make an impact on your quest for success. There is always risk. In climbing, weather is the standard wild card: it can only be predicted to a point and, as Krakauer's story underscores, can swiftly change at high elevations. Regardless of how relentlessly you prepare for the possibility of bad weather, you cannot entirely control your luck with it. And again, luck will have the final say.

The same phenomenon applies to business. You need to do everything you can to be prepared to reach your vision, but outside circumstances will have an impact on your business. The "economic weather" can change suddenly, as can environmental factors. And the literal weather flaunts its power even here as a luck maker or breaker in people attaining their goals.

For example, in North Central Washington State, there is a charming Bavarian village called Leavenworth. Over the years, its economic base has largely shifted from logging and fruit to tourism, with July and August marking the high tourist season. In 1994, that season got off to an excellent start. However, prevailing hot and dry weather soon transformed the forests around the village into dangerous tinder. When a massive thunderstorm hit in late July, this major fire threat crossed the line into disaster.

Lightning strikes ignited dozens of fires, which, within days, were blazing through the forests around Leavenworth. In the village, smoke nearly turned day into night, driving out visitors and effectively ending the high tourist season a month early. Talk about bad luck. Many business owners in Leavenworth, including a hotel owner I knew, watched one of their best months of the year go up in that smoke.

Whether you are mountaineering or managing a business, luck will thus enter into the equation. It can help or hinder you. In either event, you need to prepare your team for the ravages that bad luck could bring.

Dealing with the Luck Dilemma

The Boy Scout motto "Be prepared" succinctly captures the tenor of my advice when it comes to handling the dilemma of luck. In mountaineering, being prepared means having at a minimum 10 items known as the "10 essentials":

1. A map
2. A compass
3. A flashlight and/or headlamp (with extra batteries)
4. An extra day's food
5. Extra clothing
6. Rain gear (jacket and pants, in any climate)
7. First-aid supplies (including extra medication you are taking or might need in an emergency)
8. A pocket knife

9. Matches or a butane lighter (with extras stored in a
   watertight container)

10. Fire starter (e.g., candles, chemical fire starter, small fire logs)

Businesses too have tools and provisions that are integral to their
preparation. These might include (1) adequate capital, (2) marketable
products or services, (3) a strong sales team, (4) information technology and infrastructure, (5) physical security, and (6) strong
leadership. Foremost among the necessary tools is the SWOT
analysis, an effective strategic-planning device that was detailed
in Chapter 3.

A SWOT analysis minimizes luck's negative effects by helping you
carefully consider the opportunities and threats associated with your
business. To recap:

• Opportunities are circumstances or situations advantageous for
  your business to pursue or factor into planning.

• Threats are signs of possible or impending danger to your
  business.

To be fully prepared, you need to focus on both these areas:
opportunities, with their potential positive outcomes, as well
as threats, with their potential negative impact. That said, many
businesses have inherent vulnerabilities that make attention to
threats all the more important.

For instance, most businesses have some form of seasonality to
them; they have a more productive season and a less productive
season. The seasonality itself creates a situation where the business
is much more vulnerable to outside disruptions or threats.
Leavenworth is an extreme example of that. Seasonal businesses
need to be hyper-alert to what they can do to deal with threats.

In the case of the Leavenworth hotel owner, a prior SWOT analysis
could have made a crucial difference in the degree to which the fire

affected his business. The analysis would have shown him that
the seasonal nature of his business was so extreme that even a
temporary disruption at the wrong time, such as August, would be
a real problem. Then, in his post-analysis planning, he could have
established some defined steps to reduce his vulnerability to the
threat. Those steps might have included:

- Adding meeting rooms to the hotel. This would have allowed
  the hotel to attract convention and meeting-type businesses,
  and to expand into the shoulder seasons of May, June,
  September, and October.
- Diversifying geographically. For instance, the owner might have
  purchased another hotel in the California market, which has a
  winter tourist season. This would also provide timing diversity.

These are just two options of several that would have prepared the
owner and strengthened him against the bad luck of a short-term
disruption in his prime season.

When you consider *your* business and the luck factor, be sure to do
the following:

- Take your opportunities and threats analysis to the next level:
  envision all the scenarios that could occur and precisely what
  it would take to deal with them.
- Discuss your thoughts on this subject with your business coach
  if you have one. That person may be able to draw on some
  experience similar to yours and give you guidance on how to
  deal with the types of threats you are facing.

Of course, prepare as much as you can. Although you cannot
entirely control luck, you'll have a better chance of success if you're
adequately ready to respond to it. If it raises its good head, you'll be
more likely to grab the opportunity; if it raises its bad one, you'll be
more able to pop the threat back down.

Luck—A Fact of Life

We need to realize that regardless of how relentlessly we prepare, we don't control everything. It would be egotistical and misguided to think we somehow could. Scott Fisher and Rob Hall, two climbers who perished on Mount Everest in May 1996, were celebrated and experienced mountaineers. To say their previous successful expeditions were good luck is not completely accurate; but to say that their final expedition was bad luck is true. That storm could not have come at a worse time for them.

Samuel Goldwyn's comment "The harder I work, the luckier I get" definitely applies here. Goldwyn felt that although luck was a component of his success, the true driving component was hard work and relentless preparation. In order to maximize the effects of good luck and minimize the effects of bad luck, you need to consider both and prepare for both. If good luck befalls you, how will you capitalize on it? By the same token, if back luck hits you, how will you counter it?

Most people who are successful have had some good luck along the way; but many have had bad luck as well, and recovered and learned from it. They continued to persevere and move forward.

Chapter Ten:
Reaching Your Summit

It seems to me that people have vast potential. Most people can do extraordinary things if they have the confidence or take the risks. Yet most people don't. They sit in front of the telly and treat life as if it goes on forever.

—Philip Adams

In order for people to be happy, sometimes they have to take risks. It's true these risks can put them in danger of being hurt.

—Meg Cabot

Just do it.

—Nike marketing slogan

When I returned home from Mount Kilimanjaro, my summit climb attracted local publicity, and for a while, I was a minor celebrity. Excited by my success, many people told me, "Yeah, I would really like to do that myself!" Climbing the mountain was a feat they had thought about before, and they considered it a worthy pursuit. But that didn't mean they were poised to act on it. I was familiar with this kind of reaction from doing the ironman in my town's Ridge to River multisport race event. People would say, "Yeah, I've always wanted to do that! I should get ready to run the race next year!" But when "next year" came, these people would be saying the same thing.

Wanting to do something and doing it are not the same thing, as Nike's slogan "Just do it!" implies. Ideas and dreams are a dime a dozen, but people who truly act on them and achieve their vision are in the minority. For every person who summits Mount Kilimanjaro, there are undoubtedly thousands of people who fantasize about doing it. The fact is, you will never reach a mountaintop by merely thinking about it; nor will you reach your summit in business only by saying, "I've always wanted to do that" or "I'll do it next year."

Taking the Leap into Action

What is the key to being a doer rather than just a dreamer? Focused action. You have to decide what you want to do and then *move forward* in executing it.

This concept is essential to business. In *The E-Myth Revisited,* Michael Gerber (1995) details what he calls the entrepreneurial seizure. He describes the typical entrepreneur as a person who previously was an employee doing some type of technical work such as carpentry, engineering, accounting, or sales. Whatever the specific job, the person was probably good at it—and doing it for somebody else. Then at some point the thought struck, "I could do this better, cheaper, faster—and make more money, have more free time, and have nobody telling me what to do—if I were in my own business." That is the entrepreneurial seizure.

Once seized in this way, many people simply shrug it off, saying, "Nah, I'm comfortable where I'm at. I'll be okay." But others gather their energy and take the leap into the void. They deal with the issues that confront them, working their way to the next level of progress: owning a business. They develop a bold vision along the way and are willing to move forward, risking it all for that entrepreneurial sense that gives them immense satisfaction. These are people to be emulated.

That said, it's important to understand that risk is typically more calculated than blind in business—or any serious pursuit. Successful people are brave, but they are rarely foolhardy. In gathering energy for any leap, listen to your advisors, spouse or partner, and friends. Solicit their opinions. Carefully consider what they tell you.

For example, as I mentioned in Chapter 7, before climbing Mount Rainier—my first mountain—I took a course from Rainier Mountaineering. Its instructor taught us self-arrest and other safety lessons, all of which were invaluable. Yet perhaps of more meaning to me was his repeated advice not to be dissatisfied if we were unable to reach 14,400 feet: Rainier's absolute top. Weather, injury, and other factors could end the climb at 10,000 feet. In such a case, he said, we should consider 10,000 feet to be our mountain.

Since I had no climbing experience, I was quite unsure about my ability to get to the summit, and thought 10,000 feet would be fine. If I got to the 10,000-foot level, I'd buy a poster of the mountain, cut it off at that level, and say, "That's my Mount Rainier." Of course, as it turned out, the poster-cutting was unnecessary: conditions were favorable and I did reach the top. However, the instructor's advice perfectly addressed my initial uncertainty, deepening my determination as well as emphasizing the need for safety. As long as I went as high as possible without taking foolhardy chances and jeopardizing my life, I could still achieve my summit.

In business, most threats do not endanger your life, but rather, the life of your business. You must carefully analyze potential threats and decide if you need to cut off your mountain a bit short of your original summit. If you ignore such a need and go for that summit anyway and fail, it can cost you the entire business. Always be prepared to adjust your vision. Stay aware of where you are on your journey, and remember the option of "resting" a business at a challenging but safe level, rather than unwisely, and inflexibly, forging ahead into hazardous territory.

In the end, it's *your* decision whether you start a business, climb a mountain, or accept any other challenge you might be thinking of taking on. Recognize that you must do it on your own and that it will require diligent work as well as vigilance to threats. And then don't hold back. Go for it. Pursue your dream with a relentless passion, and stay on top of your progress. Summit the mountain—whether it's a new business you want to start or a high level of improvement in the business you already own or manage.

Questions to Take with You to the Summit

Consider the state of your business today as you would a mountain-climbing expedition, and think about the eight keys to the summit presented in this book. Focus on the following questions:

1. **Vision**
   —What is your vision for the business?
   —Where is your summit?

2. **SWOT Analysis**
   —What strengths can you capitalize on as you move forward?
   —What weaknesses are holding you back?
   —What opportunities and threats should you pay attention to?

3. Planning and Preparation

—How well have you planned for the bid for the summit?

—How can you relentlessly prepare for the bid for the summit?

—Do you have the tools and assets necessary to reach the summit?

4. Your Own Story Writing

—Are you willing to keep your possibilities open and write your own story?

—Can you take constructive advice from the stories of others without losing focus and getting discouraged?

5. A Supportive Team

—Are there any weak players on the team who need shoring up?

—Are members well prepared to work together to ensure everyone's safety and get as many people as possible on the summit?

—Are you adequately "roped" together?

6. An Experienced Guide

—Do you have a coach who will help guide you through the process?

—Is there a mentor or coach available who could help you identify the risks ahead of you and get you prepared for them?

—If you are the coach, are you prepared for that job?

7. Taking It One Step at a Time

—Do you have the appropriate key performance indicators or metrics in place?

—Have you tested these to see whether they are leading indicators or lagging ones?

—Do they have a "balanced scorecard" component to them, or are they strictly financial?

8. Luck

—Have you considered the nature of your business and any "invitations" to bad luck that may need addressing?

—Are you prepared to capitalize on good luck and counter the effects of bad luck along the way?

Whether you're "climbing the mountain" of running your own business or managing a company or department, you will be far more likely to reach your summit if you make these eight keys part of your standard equipment. So take the extra time to make sure your company is properly prepared for the future and that everyone in your expedition understands the importance of these keys. There's no question your success will be magnified as a result.

References and Resources

Bass, D., Wells, F., & Ridgeway, R. (1986). *The Seven Summits*. New York: Warner Books, Inc.

Bethune, G., & Hueler, S. (1998). *From Worst to First: Behind the Scenes of Continental's Comeback*. New York: John Wiley & Sons, Inc.

Child, G. (1993). *Mixed Emotions: Mountaineering Writings of Greg Child*. Seattle, WA: The Mountaineers.

Gerber, M. (1995). *The E-Myth Revisited: Why Most Small Businesses Don't Work and What to do About it* (rev. ed.). New York: Harper Business.

Gerstner, L. V., Jr. (2002). *Who Says Elephants Can't Dance? Inside IBM's Historic Turnaround*. New York: Harper Collins.

Horan, J. (2004). *The One Page Business Plan: Start with a Vision, Build a Company!* (3rd ed.). Berkeley, CA: The One Page Business Plan Company.

Kaplan, R. S., & Norton, D. P. (1996). *Balanced Scorecard*. Boston: Harvard Business School Press.

Krakauer, J. (1997). *Into Thin Air*. New York: Villard Books.

Porter, M. (1996, November–December). What is strategy? *Harvard Business Review*, 61–78.

Tuckman, B. W. (1965). Developmental sequences in small groups. *Psychological Bulletin, 63,* 384–399.

Ullman, J. R. (1955). *Man of Everest: The Autobiography of Tenzig Norgay*. London: George G. Harris and Co.